HOW TO DEVELOP A PRICING STRATEGY

BUSINESS SKILLS FOR EDITORS: 6

Louise Harnby

Copyright © 2020 Louise Harnby

The right of Louise Harnby to be identified as the author of this work has been asserted by her in accordance with the Copyright, Designs and Patents Act 1988. All rights reserved. This book is sold subject to the condition that it shall not, by way of trade or otherwise, be lent, re-sold, hired out or otherwise circulated in any form of binding or cover other than that in which it is published and without a similar condition including this condition being imposed on the subsequent purchaser.

ISBN: 9798664218039

CONTENTS

1. Introduction: A healthy pricing mindset	1
This guide's purpose	1
Pricing obligations and rights	1
Pricing is a journey	1
2. Different pricing strategies	3
Why pricing needn't be stressful	3
Framing pricing in terms of strategy	3
Cost-based pricing	3
Competitor-based pricing	4
Value-based pricing	4
Penetration pricing	5
Discount pricing	5
Customer-based pricing	5
Risk-based pricing	5
Democratic pricing	6
Inconvenience pricing	6
Tiered pricing	7
Client-offer pricing	7
Other options	8
A note on predatory pricing	8
3. What's the best strategy for you?	10
Factors that influence strategy choice	10
What are your business goals?	10
Which type of service/product do you offer?	11
At what career stage are you?	12
How visible are you in your ideal market?	13
Which types of clients do you work with?	14
How client-focused is your brand?	14

Which personality traits might affect your pricing decisions?	15
Which causes, philosophies and movements are you aligned with?	15
How much work do you have?	16
How important is your income's contribution to your household's welfare?	17
Case study: The pricing-strategy journey	17

4. What's the 'right' price? 21
    Subjective language and editorial pricing 21
    How currency affects pricing comparisons 21
    How circumstances affect pricing comparisons 22
    How strategy affects pricing comparisons 25
    Why lower-paying jobs can be opportunities 26

5. How to work out your minimum price 29
    Starting at the baseline 29
    A better way of defining an acceptable price 29
    Calculating the required rate – what we need to know 30
    Discovering the required rate – what's not relevant 32
    Can we go lower than our required rate? 33

6. Tracking your data 35
    Why collect data? 35
    What to record and discover 35
    Tools for the job 37

7. Communicating the price 39
    The different approaches 39
    Per word 39
    Per hour 40
    Per page 42
    Flat rate 43
    Daily rate 44

8. Build a quote that converts	46
Getting the message right	46
Why quoting is part of marketing and branding	46
How to add value to the quote	49
Framing quotes in terms of what the author saves	52
9. Going public with pricing	53
Transparency or privacy?	53
Advantages	53
Disadvantages	54
How to make your prices public	56
A not-so-public alternative: The fast ballpark price	56
Overcoming anxiety about public prices	60
Case study – the emotionality of pricing	61
10. Strategies for increasing prices	64
How strong is our position?	64
Avoiding knee-jerk thinking	65
Strategy choices: The price-acceptor	66
Strategy choices: The price-setter	67
Key factors	68
11. Why the 'race to the bottom' argument is flawed	70
Competing with cheap	70
All clients are not the same	70
Every teacup has a saucer	71
Being an Apple editor	72
12. Protecting yourself	74
Language problems: 'Delay'	74
Language problems: 'Deposit'	74
Booking forms and contracts	75
Language problems: 'Booking form'	75

The devil in the detail	76
Spotting red flags	76
13. No price is perfect	78
Appendix 1: Terms and conditions template	79
Terms and conditions: Contract of proofreading/editing services	79
Appendix 2: Privacy policy template	85
Privacy policy	85
Resources	89
Glossary of pricing strategies	91

1. Introduction: A healthy pricing mindset

This guide's purpose

This guide will show you how to develop a pricing strategy that focuses on you and your business, and that is proactive rather than reactive. The approach you take will be based on your needs, your preferences, and your circumstances.

You won't find me preaching to you about what you should charge or how you should charge. Instead, I'll guide you through the options so that you can make informed decisions based on what you feel comfortable with now. Then, if you want to make changes later because your business has grown or shifted, you can review alternative approaches with confidence.

Pricing obligations and rights

Because we're self-employed business owners, we're obliged to take responsibility for the fees we charge and accept. That will feel burdensome for some, even anxiety-inducing. But it can also be liberating when it's founded on a core belief in our right to choose.

And we do have the right to choose. No one else can or should make our pricing decisions for us because no one else has enough relevant information to make an informed assessment of what's appropriate.

We also have the right to price as we wish without shame or fear, regardless of whether others – fellow editors and clients – consider us too cheap or too expensive. No editor can claim to have found the Goldilocks pricing model – the one that's just right; there are too many variables. That's worth remembering every time you feel anxious, every time you feel judged, every time you feel unsure about your prices.

Pricing is a journey

Just because we choose a particular pricing model now doesn't mean it has to stay that way. Our pricing strategy, like every other part of our business, can and should evolve as we learn new skills, grow in confidence, become more visible, shift our focus, and expand our client lists.

What works for us today might need tweaking in a week, a month or a year. We can change our pricing approach whenever we wish – not just the fees themselves but also the terms of payment, the methods of payment, the way in which we communicate our fees to clients, the deposits we take, and the discounts we offer.

Pricing is therefore a journey. The path we take is more likely to be long and winding rather than linear. That doesn't mean we've made mistakes; it means we're prepared to try things out, review the results, and make informed decisions about whether to stay on that path or explore a new avenue.

It's my hope that by the time you've finished reading this guide, you'll feel empowered to make pricing decisions that you're comfortable with, regardless of what anyone else thinks.

2. Different pricing strategies

Why pricing needn't be stressful

Pricing is *the* topic most likely to stress out editors – newbies and old hands alike. We worry about getting it wrong, making a mistake, about undercharging and overcharging. Perhaps impostor syndrome and fear are holding our prices down. Or maybe blind arrogance or a lack of awareness are pushing our prices too high. Perhaps we're fumbling business owners and naive decision makers who are either over-ambitious, or too scared to price appropriately.

If you think that sounds like you, let me tell you right now that you are none of those things.

Framing pricing in terms of strategy

Regardless of the price you decide to offer, there is a **reason** behind it and a **name** that describes your approach, one that will be recognized throughout the global business world.

You might not yet know what your preferred strategy is called, or realize that it's even a thing strategically. This knowledge and recognition will help reframe your thinking such that every time a critic calls you out on your choice (and that critic might be you), you can justify your decision in business terms.

What follows are brief descriptions of the most oft-applied pricing strategies.

Cost-based pricing

The business owner makes something and sells it for more than the costs of production, thus making a profit.

Even editors who offer only services, not products, can assign a 'production' value to the cost of their time. Bear in mind that any single project might have the same service name as another (e.g. a copyedit) but will have a different 'production' cost. Compare the following: a light copyedit for a social science publisher; an intensive copyedit for an oncologist whose second language is English; a stylistic copyedit, which some might call a line edit, for a beginner novelist; and a time-consuming copyedit for a post-graduate student whose reference lists are muddled.

Competitor-based pricing

The business owner assesses what their competitors are charging, and prices similarly. This can be a useful and sensible first step, though editors should be aware that in reality it's difficult to implement with any certainty for the following reasons:

- Lots of editors choose not to be transparent about their pricing, which makes it impossible to establish a going market rate.
- Editors define their services differently. Two editors might both charge X per hour for editing, but one includes two passes, the other only one. That makes comparisons problematic.
- Some editors have variable rates for a single service depending on the specifics of the project (see the copyediting example in the cost-based-pricing section above).
- Guidance from editorial associations ranges from suggested minima to figures based on reported averages. Some of the figures are woefully out of date.
- Our fellow editors operate under different circumstances, in different markets, and have different personal requirements, making useful comparisons tricky to come by.

Value-based pricing

The business owner sets their prices according to the perceived value of their products or services in the market. This can be a good choice for those with a compelling client-focused brand, one that aims to drive emotional decision-making.

Clients with an appropriate budget are prepared to pay more because they believe they will get additional value as evidenced by excellent word-of-mouth referrals, useful problem-solving content, high visibility in the search engines, and scarcity of availability.

This type of strategy is unlikely to be the first choice for a new entrant who's in the early stages of brand building, marketing and client acquisition.

Penetration pricing

The business owner temporarily offers their services at a low entry price in order to attract new clients, generate word-of-mouth referrals, expand their portfolio, and acquire testimonials.

This can be a useful short-term strategy for the new entrant who wants to get their foot in the door experience-wise, and leverage that experience to acquire other, higher-paying clients. In the longer term it's unlikely to be profitable.

Discount pricing

This is an adapted form of penetration pricing and can be a useful now-and-then tool for the more experienced business owner who wants to get the attention of a client who's acknowledged their additional value but on this occasion has a budget that's lower than the editor would usually accept. You reduce your price anyway with the aim of bringing them on board at a higher rate in the future.

Customer-based pricing

The business owner believes there's a ceiling on the price their target clients will bear, and sets their rates accordingly.

Care needs to be taken with this approach because assumptions can be flawed. Extensive market research would need to be carried out to confirm the perceived ceiling – an expensive endeavour that's more likely to reveal a lower level of price sensitivity than presumed. Furthermore, many editors work for different client types with diverse expectations about what they will pay for editing.

Risk-based pricing

The business owner's price is based not just on the value of their time but also on the risk the client attaches to *not* hiring them.

In 'Pricing Design Work & Creativity' (YouTube, 2016, https://bit.ly/3dmVdCg), Chris Do, founder of Blind, a brand strategy design consultancy in Santa Monica, discusses the idea of pricing the client (or more specifically, their perceived risk) rather than the job.

He asks a group of logo designers, 'What does it touch?' The nub of the lesson is this: a bad logo on one niche website, 10 booklets and 50 promo flyers is a different problem to a bad logo on 40 aeroplanes, 20 helicopters, 14,000 vending machines and a million mailshots. The cost of rectifying the problem is different in each of those two scenarios, and so the cost of ameliorating the risk of it happening in the first place is also different.

Democratic pricing

The price is set at a level that's purposefully designed not to exclude particular communities but is still profitable.

With a *full* democratic strategy, the business owner believes in an overall pricing model that doesn't exclude those on lower incomes, and won't create a form of wealth discrimination, particularly if the client is unlikely to earn back their investment.

With a *partial* democratic strategy, the business owner offers differential pricing as a means of taking positive action to support marginalized, underrepresented and underserved communities, and the organizations that represent them.

This can be a useful option for those who want to amplify particular peoples, movements and philosophies. And while a partial democratic strategy might seem on the surface like discount pricing, it's ideologically motivated rather than growth oriented.

Inconvenience pricing

The business owner charges a fee that's higher than their standard rate because the client wants the work done at a time or in a place that's undesirable. Examples could include the following:

- The client wants the editing squeezed into your already full schedule.
- The client wishes you to work on their premises (perhaps for the sake of security).
- The client wants the project done in a time frame requiring you to work outside your standard working day or week.

Tiered pricing

The business owner factors in economies of scale. For example, per-word prices are reduced when certain word-count thresholds are met. This can be critical for editors who work on shorter-form content in any discipline.

For example, at the time of writing in 2020, I charge £75 for a 1,000-word sample edit. That price reduces to £54.50 per 1,000 words for fiction line edits around the 5,000-word mark. Projects of 10–25K words are billed at around £45 per 1,000 words. And a full-length novel line edit of, say, 80,000 words would plummet to £30 per 1,000 words. There's variation, of course, because each project has to be assessed on its own merits, but I start the process by thinking about the size of the project and the degree to which I'll be able to introduce efficiencies.

Client-offer pricing

With the aforementioned strategies, you're a price-setter. With client-offer pricing, however, you're a price-acceptor, and must decide whether to accept or walk away. More experienced editors might be in a position to negotiate; the new entrant will likely have to take what they're given. Those who work for publishers, editing agencies, packagers and project-management agencies are more likely to be working within this model.

Even though you have little control over what you earn, bear in mind the following:

- All the client-acquisition work is done for you. That makes it popular with editors who loathe marketing.
- These client types have lots of regular work. If you build a bank of ten, you'll be able to keep your schedule full. While your profits might be lower than with, say, a value-based strategy, you won't have to bear the costs of finding work.
- Marketing takes time and effort. If your visibility is poor, the client-offer position will give you space to build your brand and marketing content in preparation for a value-based strategy further down the line if you choose.

Other options

Here are a few more strategies to consider:

- **Bundle pricing**: The business owner offers a single price for multiple services (e.g. a developmental edit, followed by a copyedit, followed by a proofread).
- **Pay-what-you-want**: The business owner asks the client for a donation of the client's choosing.
- **Loss leaders**: The business owner offers a low or no price on some services in the hope of persuading the client to buy a higher-priced service (e.g. a free sample edit that could lead to being commissioned for a full edit).
- **Retainer pricing**: The business owner charges, say, a monthly fee for a client's right to use their services for an agreed number of hours, whether or not the client actually provides them with any work.

A note on predatory pricing

Penetration and discount pricing should not be confused with predatory pricing, which is considered harmful, removes competition, and is thus illegal in many jurisdictions.

If an editor were to deliberately set their rates so low as to knock all their competitors out of the market, then raise their prices and monopolize the now empty-but-for-them editing space, that would be a predatory pricing strategy.

Regardless of how low an editor sets their fees, it will never be a predatory strategy, for these reasons:

- The client market is global and no single editor can fulfil demand.
- Clients have a multitude of specialist requirements (e.g. time constraints, subject/genre knowledge, level of editing, emotional connection to brand, language skills) and no single editor can fulfil them all.

If someone tells you that your pricing strategy is predatory, they've misunderstood the term. Kickback about perceived low pricing is more likely to come in the form of terms such as 'race to the bottom', 'underpricing' and 'undermining'. In a later chapter, we'll look in more detail at why this position is flawed.

Summing up

For every editor, there's a strategy that fits. Framing pricing decisions in terms of strategy helps bat away anxiety and impostor syndrome. It makes it easier to give ourselves permission to choose our own path, discover what works (and doesn't work), learn from experience, and make changes when our business is ready.

3. What's the best strategy for you?

Factors that influence strategy choice

There's more than one pricing strategy to fit an editor's needs. Which one(s) you choose will depend on multiple factors. Set aside some time to answer the following questions. There is more detail and guidance to help you below:

- What are your business goals?
- Which type of service/product do you offer?
- At what career stage are you?
- How visible are you in your ideal market?
- Which types of clients do you work with?
- How client-focused is your brand?
- Which personality traits might affect your pricing decisions?
- Which causes, philosophies and movements are you aligned with?
- How much work do you have?
- How important is your income's contribution to your household's welfare?

Thinking about each of these questions separately helps us navigate the issue of pricing, though in reality any walls we erect are permeable. Don't be surprised if similar themes are repeated when you carry out the exercise.

The suggestions I offer in each section are not the best and only options, just ideas to get you thinking. At the end of the guide there's a quick-reference one-page glossary of the pricing strategies I discussed in Chapter 2.

What are your business goals?

What do you want to achieve in your business? It's a broad question, and one only you can answer, but understanding what you want, what's working, and what you want to change helps you identify which strategies might work best. Since pricing is part of marketing, achieving your goals might mean adapting your promotion strategy too.

Remember, you can use multiple strategies so there's no need to limit your thinking. Here are a few ideas to get you started:

- I want to increase my monthly income.
- I want to proofread academic books and journal articles for publishers because there's less likely to be scope creep.
- I want to switch to a different market that I have no experience in.
- I want to spend less time marketing (which I dislike and takes too much time).
- I want to scale my editing business by earning passive income.
- I want a fuller/lighter schedule.

Editors who want to increase income can look at how they value an hour of their time, then rework a **cost-based** strategy. Or they can experiment with **tiered** or **bundle pricing**. Or they can create passive income products priced with **customer ceilings** in mind, or according to **cost** plus **value**.

Those who want to focus on clients in the traditional publishing industry will do well to embrace **client-offer pricing**, but with a view to building trust so that negotiation is possible.

If your goal is to have a larger book of work and a longer wait list, **bundle pricing** could attract clients seeking a full service; **client-offer pricing** would enable you to work comfortably with agencies, publishers and packagers who do all your client-acquisition work for you. However, if you want to trim your schedule but not your profitability, a **value-based** strategy could be worth experimenting with.

Which type of service/product do you offer?

What you're selling affects your choice of pricing strategy too. Think about what you currently offer *and* what you might introduce. Do you fall into one of the following categories, or something else?

- I offer in-house proofreading training for corporates.
- I offer proofreading/copyediting for corporates.
- I offer novel critiques.
- I offer book-coaching.
- I offer self-directed training to other editors.

- I offer business coaching to other editors.
- I offer copyediting services for publishers.

Editors who scale their businesses and offer products such as courses, books, guides, webinars, apps and tools can consider a **cost-based strategy** as a guide to their minimum price. You might also have a sense of the maximum price your audience will pay for your product (e.g. no more than £x for a guide; no more than £x for a self-directed course; no more than £x for a mentored course; no more than £x per hour for coaching), in which case you can use a **customer-based** strategy. **Bundle pricing** – a lower total price for multiple purchases – is also worth testing, as is short-term **discount pricing** (e.g. early-bird, pre-launch or prepublication).

Editors who offer only services might prefer multiple strategies:

- Client-offer pricing for publishers
- Value-based pricing for online leads
- **Inconvenience** or **risk-based pricing** for corporates and comms agencies
- Partial democratic pricing for not-for-profits
- Tiered pricing for students
- **Bundle pricing** for clients seeking a full service
- **Cost-based pricing** for independent authors and academics

At what career stage are you?

Career stage is relevant because it determines how much practical experience we have, which in turn affects the degree to which we can signal to a potential client that we're worth a price. Which of the following resonates with you?

- I'm a new entrant to the field.
- I'm in the middle of my career.
- My business is mature.
- My existing business is middle-stage or mature but I'm looking to switch disciplines or services.

New entrants who want to gain experience might consider **loss-leader pricing** (such as free sample edits) and short-term **penetration pricing** to build their portfolios. While I advise caution with this approach, I still believe it has its place, as long as the client is aware that the offer is special and time-limited. Ensure you leverage the opportunity to its max by, for example, asking for a testimonial and featuring the project in your portfolio. You might even ask the author to contribute to some form of content collaboration, such as doing a podcast or blog interview with you.

Middle-stage and mature editors seeking to switch disciplines could experiment with **penetration pricing**. However, since they have a wealth of experience to leverage, they might prefer a strategy that takes into account the following:

- How they value their time (e.g. **cost-based pricing**).
- How strong their brand is (e.g. **value-based pricing**).
- What type of clients they work for (e.g. **client-offer pricing** if they work for publishers).
- What their personality type is (e.g. **competitor-based pricing** if they're cautious).
- What their values are (e.g. **democratic pricing**).
- What they're working on (e.g. **tiered pricing** for variable word counts).

How visible are you in your ideal market?

How visible we are to our ideal clients, and the degree to which that visibility feeds into our desired income, affects our pricing choices. Do any of the following statements describe your situation?

- I'm visible to my ideal clients and comfortable with what I earn from them.
- I'm visible to my ideal clients but unhappy with what I'm earning.
- I'd like to be visible to a particular client group but I've yet to implement any plans.

Editors who are visible but want to earn more could introduce **value-based** or **tiered pricing** into the mix. The former will deter poorer-fit lower-paying clients; the latter enables them to increase profits for shorter-form content.

Editors who are invisible might try **bundle, loss-leader, penetration** and **discount pricing** strategies in order to get traction in their ideal market.

Which types of clients do you work with?

Our client-types choices will affect the prices we are offered, the prices we charge, and the price expectations. Who do you work with? Who do you *want* to work with? How will that affect your pricing?

- I work with publishers.
- I work with charities and causes I believe in.
- I work with agencies who need a fast turnaround.
- I work with students whose second language is English.
- I work with big brands on materials that will be widely publicized.

Editors with clients for whom errors in the text would have a significantly higher negative impact than is standard might consider a **risk-based pricing** strategy.

Those who work with agencies representing wealthy corporates and who need a fast turnaround might choose an **inconvenience pricing** strategy or a **retainer pricing** strategy.

Editors who work with publishers and packagers might have no other option but to accept **client-offer pricing**. This isn't a given in all publishing sectors, but it's more likely than not.

And those who work with charities could introduce **partial democratic pricing**.

How client-focused is your brand?

Our messaging – the way we make our target clients feel – affects their trust in us. Buying our services becomes emotional. The stronger our brand, the more we have control over our price. Which of the following sounds like you?

- I've invested time in developing a distinct online brand identity that's client-focused.
- I'm still working on this element of my business.
- I'm not sure what branding is or why it's relevant.
- I know what branding is but have no interest in developing it.

Editors who already work for publishers and packagers might be able to negotiate **client-offer prices** because trust in their ability is so high.

Those working with independent academics and novelists, and who are known and trusted in their field, are in a stronger position to use **value-based pricing**.

Those who are still developing trust and whose brands have yet to gain traction might feel more comfortable with **competitor-based pricing** in the main, but could also experiment with some short-term **penetration pricing** to get attention. **Bundle pricing** could be an attractive proposition for clients with limited budgets but who want a full service.

Which personality traits might affect your pricing decisions?

Personality can affect pricing decisions, particularly those that feel risky. What traits might interfere with or drive your pricing strategy?

- I'm introverted but I'll try new things anyway.
- I'm a confident, outgoing self-starter.
- I don't like being the centre of attention.
- I like to take things steady.

Editors who like stability and loathe marketing might enjoy the security of **client-offer pricing** from publishers and packagers, and choose **cost-based pricing** for their non-publisher clients. Those who like to follow the crowd might choose **competitor-based pricing** until they have more confidence in their own brand and acquire a more secure client base. They could also experiment with **bundle** or **tiered pricing**.

Confident self-starters might experiment with the likes of **penetration** and **discount pricing** if they're expanding their services or accessing new markets; **value-based pricing** if they're actively content marketing; or **risk-based** and **inconvenience pricing** if they're targeting markets where written materials are brand- or time-sensitive.

Which causes, philosophies and movements are you aligned with?

Sometimes it's not just about the money. Yes, our businesses need to pay for themselves, but our belief systems can play a part in how we operate too. There are many ways to give, to support, to engage. They needn't be connected with our editing work, but they can be. They needn't be solely about pricing – training, education and engagement are important too – but they can be. Where do you stand?

- I'm actively involved with one or more marginalized, underrepresented or underserved communities and want this reflected directly in my pricing.
- I support a number of charities and not-for-profits, and I'm interested in how I might align this with my business.
- I keep politics and charitable donations separate from business.

A **democratic pricing** strategy, either full or partial, is the tool of choice for editors who want to integrate ideology into their business. It's action on the front end; it also affects profitability on the front end.

For those who are more risk-averse, supporting at the back end – via donations or other types of engagement – will offer more flexibility.

How much work do you have?

How full the cupboard is and how quickly we need to fill it will affect pricing decisions. We can use different strategies to solve shorter- and longer-term problems. How healthy is your book of work?

- I have as much work as I need, but I'd like to earn more.
- I have as much work as I need and I'm happy with what I'm earning.
- I do have work but I often worry about what my schedule will look like in a few weeks' time.
- My cupboard is bare.

Editors who have plenty of work and a long wait list (thereby demonstrating scarcity) can experiment with **value-based pricing** in the knowledge that time is on their side if fee increases hurt bookings.

Editors who are concerned about their workstream might consider refocusing their marketing strategy and contacting publishers and packagers. **Client-offer pricing** is the likely outcome, and could result in lower than desired rates, but being self-unemployed nullifies control over pricing anyway. Sourcing a bank of clients who can supply regular work removes stress and stabilizes the business while the editor develops a marketing strategy to attract clients who will pay more.

How important is your income's contribution to your household's welfare?

Those of us whose households rely on our income will have to think more cautiously about pricing decisions if a change in strategy comes with risk. Transitional approaches might be more effective for some. Think about where your income stands in relation to your household's welfare:

- My income is essential to my household.
- My income is welcome but we could just about survive without it if we had to.
- My income is what pays for luxuries.
- My income is irrelevant.

Editors whose income doesn't impact on their household's ability to thrive have more options because there's no risk to experimenting with pricing strategies. However, many of us work to thrive not just emotionally but economically too. That means understanding our baseline required rate so that at the very least a **cost-based pricing** strategy is profitable.

Steady income from clients who set the prices (**client-offer pricing**) can provide a good buffer for editors whose income is essential or welcome, but who in the longer term would like to do one of the following:

- Phase in better-paying clients with a **value-based pricing** and marketing strategy.
- Experiment with **tiered** or **bundle pricing**.
- Develop relationships with clients for whom an **inconvenience** or **retainer pricing** model is a good fit.

Case study: The pricing-strategy journey

This case study offers an overview of how my own pricing strategy has developed since I set up my business in 2006, and how as I write this guide in 2020, I'm still using more than one approach when I need to.

2006: New entrant to the field

Following my initial training (I undertook what's now The Publishing Training Centre's 'Essential Proofreading'), I decided to contact several small independent publishers that were based locally. Owing to budget limitations, these presses did all their editorial work in-house rather than contracting out to freelancers.

I used a **penetration pricing** approach. I offered to work for free for two of these publishers, and at an artificially low price for a couple of others. The offer was framed within an explanation of my desire to gain experience and acquire testimonials that I could use to prove my worth to larger publishers.

The strategy was successful. One publisher gave me a couple of jobs and a wonderful testimonial. A year later, during a busy period, they hired me (and paid me). The project experience and testimonial were also directly responsible for my being hired for proofreading by an academic publisher on a regular basis for nearly a decade thereafter.

2006–2012: Building my business

During this period, I had a young child. While our household had already adjusted to making ends meet without my former office-based income, things were tight so I was keen to acquire a regular bank of clients as soon as I could. For that reason, I focused on a market that had its hand raised – publishers.

Nearly all my clients were academic presses. I also worked regularly for a project-management agency. These clients had freelance budgets and fixed rates for proofreading and copyediting.

Since I was a price-acceptor, the **client-offer pricing** model was in play. It suited me perfectly. I was balancing business development with bringing up a young child, and while my business wasn't as profitable as it is now, I spent far less time on marketing than I do now because the presses and the PM agency were doing all my client-acquisition work for me. I believe it was a fair exchange.

On occasion, I'd negotiate with these clients if I believed the project warranted it. Sometimes I was successful, sometimes I wasn't, but the option was certainly there once my clients had learned to trust me.

2012–2017: Becoming discoverable

In 2012, I had begun my blogging journey. It would be several years before I'd define my brand clearly and integrate my marketing strategy fully into what I'd discover during my branding journey, but my visibility in the search engines improved significantly and independent authors and scholars began to find me.

With these clients, I was a price-setter rather than a price-acceptor. Because I had little sense beyond the publishing industry of what these clients would pay, I did the best I could with **competitor-based pricing**. I used the now Chartered Institute of Editing and Proofreading's suggested minimum rates as a guideline and kept an eye on the discussions in the Facebook forums. I came away from those discussions convinced that there was an editor for every budget, and more confident about going my own way based on my personal needs and wants.

On several occasions, I introduced a **risk-based strategy** (proofreading text that would be printed on 80,000 greetings cards) and an **inconvenience pricing strategy** (for a comms agency working on behalf of a public-services ombudsman who wanted my editing services fast and outside my prescribed working hours).

The shift in my client base was gradual, which gave me the opportunity to phase out steady work from some of my lower-paying publishers.

2017–present: The visible editor

In 2017, I began working intensively on developing the following:

- Fiction line-craft skills
- A strong brand that focused on attracting my ideal clients – fiction authors

The outcome of this was a decision to specialize in sentence-level fiction editing, and the creation of content that would add value for those clients.

As I gained skills and confidence, I shifted to **value-based pricing**. My brand and marketing continued to work hard for me so that my wait list grew from three months in 2017 to six months in 2018, to a year by 2019, to fifteen months by 2020. That gave me a buffer in which to experiment with price increases, safe in the knowledge that I could make adjustments if my price points missed the mark.

That's where I am today. I'm not in the slightest bit interested whether other editors think I'm too cheap or too expensive. Furthermore, if an author considers me too expensive, that's no problem; we're just not a good fit.

Value-based pricing is my primary strategy but, once in a while, I will consider **discount pricing**. In 2020, a client asked for proofreading. They'd already invested in a professional copyedit but the sample indicated there was still a lot of stylistic work required to make the book ready for market. Their budget precluded this, though they made it clear that they saw the value in me and my services, based on my website.

Because I wanted this client to pick me as their line editor next time around, I offered to work at an artificially low price on this occasion so I could show this author what I could do. While there was a risk the strategy would backfire, it was one I was prepared to shoulder. It paid off. They hired me for their next line edit at my published price.

I also use **tiered pricing** that differentiates between projects with over 30,000 words and projects with smaller word counts (e.g. sample edits and short stories).

I don't offer **democratic pricing** but do make donations to several not-for-profits that actively seek to amplify the presence of marginalized communities through the world of words.

Finally, I offer books, shorter guides, and multimedia courses for editors. I've chosen a hybrid strategy for this arm of my business: **democratic, cost-based** and **customer-based pricing**.

Summing up

Different strategies can be employed at different career stages, with different client types, and in different situations. The choice you make will also reflect your own preferences and strengths. I love marketing my business, am passionate about the power of branding, and enjoy the challenge of being visible on Google. But that's me. If you're someone who prefers to devote time to other aspects of your business and life, a **client-offer strategy** might appeal. And while I've been in business since 2006, you might be starting out, in which case navigating **competitor-based** and **penetration pricing** might appeal.

There's no right or wrong, just different options. Choose what works for you, regardless of what anyone else says, and feel free to try something new when the time feels right. If someone (including you) kicks back on your decision, remind them that this is your professional *strategy*, one that you have the right to choose, review and adapt as you see fit because it's your business, not theirs – literally.

4. What's the 'right' price?

Subjective language and editorial pricing

Terms like 'good', 'high' and 'fair', and 'low', 'poor' and 'predatory' are problematic because they're used by individual freelancers to reflect their *own* experiences and circumstances, which are often very different. It's critical that we recognize the subjectivity in play during rates discussions.

Although it can be interesting to hear colleagues' opinions of whether a fee is good or bad, or high or low, or amazing or insulting, their views won't help us determine how we need to price our work because it's only our circumstances that are relevant.

This chapter demonstrates why editors need to be wary of paying too much heed to other people's views on their pricing, particularly when it comes to client-offer and competitor-based strategies.

How currency affects pricing comparisons

Currency, especially currency fluctuations, make rates comparisons virtually impossible. Here's an example to illustrate the problem.

The American proofreader

Proofreader A lives in Oxnard, CA, USA. She tells her colleagues in an online forum that she's accepted an offer from an agency to proofread 4,000 words for US$25. She estimates the job will take an hour. Some of her US colleagues say the rate is unacceptably low; some even believe that she's encouraging a race to the bottom by accepting such a fee from an organization whose rates are clearly unfair.

The British proofreader

Meanwhile, Proofreader B, who lives in Manchester, UK, is reading the forum thread.

- If it were 2015, the exchange rate is 1 GBP = 1.5328 USD. US$25 converts to £16.31.

- If it were 2016, some months before the UK's referendum on membership of the European Union, the exchange rate is 1 GBP = 1.4686 USD. US$25 converts to £17.02.
- If it were 2020, when the world was in the middle of a global pandemic, and the pound had crashed to its worst rate in thirty years, the exchange rate is 1 GBP = 1.1764 USD. US$25 converts to £21.25.

There are already significant differences between these rates, but let's also imagine that none of the scenarios above is reality. Instead, let's say the pound has collapsed beyond even the worst expectations because of some awful thing or another, and 1 GBP = 0.8 USD, which means that US$25 converts to £31.25.

Proofreader B needs to earn a minimum of £20 an hour to meet her needs.

- If it's January 2015 or 2016, she thinks the agency's rate looks low because she has enough clients filling her schedule who're paying a fee of a little over £20 per hour. The agency work therefore holds no appeal for her and she dismisses any thoughts of working with them.
- If it's 2020, she thinks the agency's rate is okay, but she already has enough clients filling her schedule who are paying that fee so she doesn't feel compelled to jump through the hoops to get on board.
- If it's our made-up world, she's already working out how she'll word her email to the agency before she's finished reading the thread. She thinks it's a fantastic opportunity!

Notice how as the exchange rate fluctuates, so do Proofreader B's perceptions of whether a price is high, okay or low.

How circumstances affect pricing comparisons

Personal circumstances make rates comparisons equally difficult. Here's another example.

Proofreader C

Proofreader C lives in Belfast, Northern Ireland. She tells her colleagues in an online forum that she's accepted an offer from an agency to proofread 4,000 words for £16. She estimates the job will take an hour.

Some of her colleagues say that the rate is unacceptably low; some even believe that she's encouraging a race to the bottom by accepting such a fee from an organization whose rates are clearly unfair.

Proofreader D

Meanwhile, Proofreader D, who lives just down the road from C, is reading the forum thread. She's been working for a local supermarket, earning the UK's legal national living wage of £8.72 per hour for people over 25 years of age (as at April 2020). She lives at home with her parents so she's able to survive on this.

In her spare time she took an intensive distance-learning proofreading course and passed with distinction. Now she needs to find clients, acquire practical experience, build her portfolio, and get some glowing testimonials – all valuable stuff that she'll be able to leverage later with other clients.

From her perspective, every hour spent working for that agency would be an hour spent earning 84% more than if she were working in the supermarket. To her, the rate looks high.

She appreciates that the agency might not be a viable solution in the longer term, but her marketing is currently non-existent, which means her visibility to potential clients is non-existent. The agency work would ameliorate the problem while she attends to making herself discoverable. Once she's done that, she can shift away from the client-offer pricing strategy, and towards value-based pricing.

Proofreader E

Proofreader E also lives in Northern Ireland, but to the west of Belfast in Strabane. She's been professionally proofreading for eight years so her business is mature. She's a marketing monster. Her website is highly visible on Google. She's a member of the CIEP, EPANI and AFEPI, and advertises in their directories. Her portfolio's stunning, her testimonials glowing. Anyone visiting those directories or her website will be in no doubt that she's an experienced professional who can solve their problems.

Her business has grown from strength to strength. She remembers what it was like to be in D's shoes, but that's not where she is any longer. These days, all her academic and business clients find her via the search engines or her professional society directories. She no longer works for agencies, packagers or publishers, though she gladly took work from them in the early days. Now, though, her own marketing strategy brings clients directly to her.

Her hourly rate is £38 and this supplements her partner's income. The partner annually brings in 40% more than her, so her contribution means they have a comfortable lifestyle.

From her perspective, every hour spent working for that agency would be an hour spent earning 58% less than her current rate. To her, the rate looks low.

The agency is not worth a glance because she doesn't need the client-acquisition benefit that Proofreader D is attracted to, and she can earn more from the pool of clients who want to hire her at the hourly rate she's set under her value-based pricing strategy.

Proofreader F

Proofreader F lives next door to E. She's in the same boat as E except her partner was made redundant four months ago.

The agency's £16 won't cut it. Proofreader E's £38 won't cut it. She needs £115 an hour. From her perspective, anything under £115 per hour is low because that's what she requires to avoid moving to a smaller apartment, cancelling the pet insurance, junking the gym membership, throwing her Sky box into the trash, and selling the BMW. If things don't get better soon, she might have to give the pet away, or maybe the partner. She hasn't decided which yet, but the partner's food bills are higher.

Notice also that although Proofreaders D, E and F are operating within the same geographical region and the same currency market, their different circumstances also affect their perceptions of whether a given rate is low or high, and viable or not.

If we want to work out whether Agency X, Publisher Y or Packager Z's rates are acceptable, we need to know what good, high, fair, low, poor and so on mean to us based on our situation – not anyone else's. The same applies when we're deciding what price to set with clients who come directly to us.

How strategy affects pricing comparisons

Pricing strategy choices muddy the waters too. Here's a final example.

Fiction editor A

Editor A is reading a thread in a fiction-editing forum about whether to publicize rates. Two editors state that their websites include rate cards, so A goes to take a look.

Editor B charges £30 per 1,000 words for line editing, while Editor C charges £15 per 1,000 words for the same service.

B and C are both known to A. Both have strong online profiles, mature brands and lots of experience. Both offer training courses. Both have written books. Both are discussed favourably in the editing community. And yet B's advertised rates are double those of C. What's going on?

Given that these editors offer similar services, editor A thinks one of them must surely be going wrong somewhere. Their prices are so far apart that they can't *both* be pricing in a way that's viable, right, fair or whatever, can they? Is B overcharging and pricing herself out of the market, or is C undercharging and taking part in the race to the bottom? Does C not understand the value of her services, or does B have an inflated sense of her own worth?

In fact, what editor A doesn't realize is that she's raising questions based on numbers. What she doesn't know and can't factor in are B and C's pricing strategies.

Fiction editors B and C

Editor B has chosen a value-based strategy. She believes she's worth £60 per hour. Since she line edits at an average speed of 2,000 words per hour, her price is £30 per 1,000 words. Those who can't afford that price aren't her target clients. She's also booked up for fifteen months.

Editor C has chosen a full democratic strategy. She works at the same speed as B. She also believes she's worth £60 an hour. However, she doesn't want to exclude those who can't afford that. She can still remain profitable by earning £30 per hour so she sets her prices so that authors with a wider range of incomes will be able to access her editing services, and at the same time ameliorates her concerns about wealth inequality.

Editors B and C both have ideological principles, but B manages hers on the back end – via donations – while C does so at the front end via her pricing strategy.

Why lower-paying jobs can be opportunities

Running an editing or proofreading business is a journey, not a moment in time. Some of us will be offered work that's not ideal because of fee, content, client type, time frame, or some other reason. Would acceptance be a compromise or an opportunity?

Ideal editing jobs are something to aim for but not necessarily what land in our laps in the start-up phase of a business.

- Perhaps the fee is a lot lower than we'd like or than some of our editing friends are earning.
- Perhaps the subject or genre on offer isn't what we dreamed of when we set up our business.
- Perhaps the client is a publisher whereas we'd prefer to work with corporates.
- Perhaps the client wants the project completed in a time frame that means we'd have to work outside our preferred office hours.

The invisibility of being new

Being discoverable is a challenge for many new starters. Ideal projects are out there, but the editor or proofreader isn't yet visible enough in the relevant spaces. And even if they can be found, they might not yet have enough experience to instil the trust that leads to initial contact.

Broadly, it's easier to get in front of publishers because we know who and where they are. They're used to being contacted by us, too, so we can go direct and cold. With non-publishers, it's more difficult. Not every business, charity, school, indie author, or student wants an editor or understands the value we bring to the table. Going direct and cold is a trickier proposition.

It's not just the mechanics of visibility. Emotion plays a part too, especially trust. With publishers it's easier to overcome the trust barrier.

They know what they want, what we do, are used to working with us, speak our language, and are experienced in evaluating our competence.

Non-publisher clients are more of a challenge. They might not be familiar with the different levels of editing. Many won't have worked with a professional editor before. Some – for example fiction writers – might be anxious about exposing their writing to someone they don't know. And for the inexperienced client, evaluating a good fit is more difficult. In the start-up phase of business ownership, editors and proofreaders with less experience might therefore find it easier to acquire work with publishers and packagers than with non-publishers.

If visibility and trust issues mean that new entrants to the field don't always have the breadth of choice as more mature business owners, it could mean deciding to accept work that isn't ideal in the shorter term. However, that shouldn't be automatically seen as a compromise or a bad choice. It might be an opportunity. What we do this year is not separate from what will happen next year, or the year after, or five years down the road. All the choices we make on our business journey are connected.

Thinking beyond the bubble of now

Here's a story about how I accepted work that was way below my ideal price point, and did so with pleasure because I believed I'd be able to leverage it later. I hope it will reassure you if you're worrying about whether to accept a job you believe could be valuable.

Some years ago, I was commissioned to proofread several books for a publisher:

- *The Rats* – a reissue of one the first novel published by one of the UK's most well-known horror authors.
- *Dracula* – the centenary edition of possibly the most famous Gothic horror novel ever written.
- *A Visit from the Goon Squad* – a Pulitzer-prize winner.
- *Three Moments of an Explosion* – a short-story collection from China Miéville, one of the hottest 'weird' fiction talents in the market.
- Reissues of *The Stepford Wives* by Ira Levin, and *Cool Hand Luke* by Donn Pearce.

I accepted £13 per hour. Even back then, the fee was below my required hourly rate, and earned me less than half my desired hourly rate. Did I compromise?

- If I believe that each decision I make exists in the *bubble of now*, and that nothing affects anything else further down the road, then yes, I compromised.
- If I think that what I'm earning now is *despite* my decision to accept those proofreading projects, it was a massive compromise.
- But if I believe that each decision I make can affect my choices down the road, that the walls around those individual decisions are permeable, it's a different story. If I think that what I'm earning now is *because of* my decision to accept those proofreading projects, it's a story of opportunity.

Authors make decisions to work with editors based on a whole host of factors, but the first step is deciding to get in touch in the belief that the person they've found feels like a good fit.

For example, those of us who edit fiction for self-publishers are asking those authors to put their novels in the hands of complete strangers. Many of those authors have never worked with an independent editor. Some are anxious about the process of being edited. And for some, the editor's might be only the second pair of eyes to read the text. It's a big ask that takes courage. And that's where the trust comes in.

The editor who can instil trust quickly is more likely to compel authors to make the leap and hit the contact button. And what better way to instil trust than offer a portfolio of mainstream published books written by big-name authors? That's how I leveraged those half-my-ideal-fee books. They tell an anxious indie author that publishers of big-name books trusted me a few years ago. That helps the author trust me *now*.

Summing up

Other editors' pricing decisions make sense to us only when we have full information, which we rarely do. That's why our competitors are not the best guides when it comes to deciding whether a rate is good or bad, high or low, fair or unfair. By moving away from subjective evaluation and a bubble of now, and towards strategic, longer-term thinking based on data and opportunity, we're better able to price confidently and comfortably.

5. How to work out your minimum price

Starting at the baseline

Now that we understand why our colleagues' views on a particular rate don't help us make informed decisions about whether to accept a client's offer, or what price to charge if we're setting the price, it's time to delve into what *is* relevant.

There are some baseline questions we can ask and data that we can track to help us decide what to charge. Those at the beginning of their careers will have to make some educated guesses. Do your best for now. It'll become easier as you build your project portfolio.

A better way of defining an acceptable price

Instead of thinking in terms of what's right or fair, we can construct a broad definition of what's acceptable to us, and only us, by identifying the three core rates that matter:

- **Required rate**: This is what we *need* to earn in order to meet our baseline financial needs.
- **Desired rate**: This is what we *want* to earn in order to fulfil our aspirations.
- **Market rate in that moment**: This is what the *client will pay or offer* for a particular job.

Each time we're asked by a publisher, packager or other agency if we'll take on an editing project for a fee of their choosing (the market rate in that moment), we can assess it against our required and desired rates:

- Market rate is equal to or higher than our required rate = **good enough**
- Market rate is equal to or higher than our desired rate = **great**
- Market rate is lower than our required rate = **poor**

And each time we offer a price to a client (*our* market rate in the moment), we can assess it against our required and desired rates:

- Our offer is equal to or higher than our required rate = **good enough**
- Our offer is equal to or higher than our desired rate = **great**
- Our offer is lower than our required rate = **poor**

That doesn't mean we must always reject rates or lower our prices in order to secure a client. We'll look briefly at offsetting at the end of the chapter. For now, however, let's delve deeper into what we need to know to create a baseline required rate.

Calculating the required rate – what we need to know

The required rate is the first step towards understanding the value we place on our time. It is central to every editorial pricing strategy, not least cost-based fees. The equation has three key components:

- Editing speed
- Hours available for editing
- Expenditure

Editing speed

How fast can you carry out the particular type of editing? Bear in mind that not all editing is the same, even if it it's called the same thing. A copyedit for a client who's an experienced writer might need just a gentle tidy-up and quality-control check, whereas a copyedit for a less experienced writer might need extensive and time-consuming revision. The former will be quicker to edit than the latter.

Sampling is a good first step to estimating how long a project will take, not least because it gives us a worst-case scenario, which means we're less likely to undercharge (i.e. fail to meet our baseline costs of production). With lengthier projects, economies of scale will kick in once we've become familiar with the project because:

- We spot oft-repeated problems.
- We get into the flow of the writing.
- Even if recording and implementing style choices is time-consuming, we need do it only once, whether the project is 1,000 words or 100,000.

- We can used productivity tools such as macros, templates and styles.

Hours available for editing

If you need to earn £600 per week, and you have 25 hours available, you'll need to charge (or accept) at least £24 per hour.

If you have only 10 hours available, you'll need to charge (or accept) at least £60 per hour.

Even if you have 50 hours available (meaning you could drop your minimum hourly rate to £12 per hour), could you sustain it? Only you know the answer to that.

Expenditure

It matters little what you actually charge (or accept) if that number is less than the one attached to your costs of living.

For example, if a regular client pays you £300 an hour, but holding off the bailiffs means earning £350 an hour, £300 is too low. You'll need to work more hours, reduce your outgoings, or increase your prices.

In addition to the basic costs of living (food, clothes, utilities, mortgage, health insurance, and so on), there will be business costs. These include but are not limited to the following:

- Broadband and phone connection
- Domain name and website hosting
- Banking
- Reference manuals and style guides
- Computer hardware
- Software
- Training and continuing professional development
- Memberships
- Marketing tools
- Professional indemnity insurance
- Dependent care during working hours
- Pension provision
- Tax obligations

Don't forget exchange rates. If you're dealing with a client from another country, one of two situations will be in play:

- You're a price-acceptor and the client offers a project at a price they've set.
- You're a price-setter and the client asks you for a quote in their local currency.

In either case, you need to factor in the exchange rate and additional fees (e.g. bank charges, PayPal fees).

Example

Tonya is a fiction editor who's in the process of reviewing her copyediting fees. Here's a summary of her data:

A. Her contribution to the household's monthly costs of living: £1,200
B. Her monthly business costs (including estimated tax obligations): £500
C. Total costs per month = £1,700
D. Hours available for editing per month: 100
E. Average editing speed: 1,800 words per hour
F. Minimum required price per hour to break even (C/D) = £17
G. Minimum price per 1,000 words to break even (F/E x 1,000) = £9.44
H. Minimum price per word to break even (G/E) = £00.0094

F, G and H are not what Tonya *should* charge. Rather, they're the minimum *she needs to earn* in order for her business to be viable. If she wants to make a profit, she'll either need to reduce her outgoings, increase her hours or increase her prices.

It's irrelevant if another editor thinks that £17/h or £9.44/1K words is too low. All that matters is that Tonya understands how to calculate her minimum required rate, and factors that figure into the pricings strategies she chooses.

Discovering the required rate – what's not relevant

Remember, the following are interesting but not relevant to how we actually set a price (or group of prices):

- Other editors' prices
- Editors' subjective views on other editors' prices
- Clients' subjective views on what editors should charge
- National editorial societies' suggested minima

Let's revisit the Tonya example above. On one particular day, a publisher offers her a rate of £18 per hour to copyedit a novel. This rate is non-negotiable. Two hours later, an independent author requests her copyediting services.

The author's novel amplifies the voices of a community that Tonya wants to support, so although she wishes to make a profit from her editing, ideology is also a motivation. She reviews the file and offers a fee that will equate to £22 per hour, which is accepted.

At the time, her national editorial society suggests a minimum of £29.60 per hour, but that's irrelevant because Tonya's price doesn't have to meet the needs of the professional society; the professional society doesn't pay for her rent, food, and bills. Nor does it know anything about which people, groups, causes and philosophies she's connected to and motivated by. All the price needs to do is meet her minimum requirement: £17 per hour.

For every hour she works for the publisher (within a client-offer pricing strategy), she'll make a profit of £1. For every hour she works for the author (within a partial democratic pricing strategy), she'll make a profit of £5. If she's happy with those figures and can fit in both jobs, she has a business-led justification for taking both.

Other people are not responsible for running our businesses or our homes, so their opinions should not be used to determine whether we accept or decline work at a given price, nor whether we offer work at a particular price.

Can we go lower than our required rate?

Running a business isn't just about profitability; it's also about satisfaction. Consider the following scenarios:

- We want to support a particular movement or community with our editing services, and wish to remove price from the equation.
- We want to gain experience that we can leverage in a hitherto untapped market.

- Job satisfaction would be high enough to trump financial reward.

Still, our business as a whole needs to be profitable, otherwise we'll be running on empty. Building a bank of data helps us to evaluate whether offsetting is possible.

Offsetting

Back to Tonya. She wants to support a particular charity that's close to her heart. It needs 10 pages of its website checking. Tonya's desired rate for this type of work is £100 per web page; her required rate is £25 per web page.

The charity's been hit hard by a recession – donations are down 30% – and its budget is £100 in total. That's £10 per web page, way off Tonya's minimum web-page rate. She does it anyway because she wants to and because she can afford to. That's because she has new client – a Fortune 500 company who brings her on site once a month and pays her big bucks (well over her desired rate) for the inconvenience and because they value her expertise.

Tonya offsets the losses accrued to the charity work against the profits gained from the Fortune 500 company work.

Summing up

Work out the minimum price you need to earn on either an hourly or per-word basis so that your decisions about what to charge (or what fee to accept) start at a point where you're breaking even.

If you're already completing tax returns, you'll have a good chunk of your business-expenditure data. If you're at the start of your editing career, and you've yet to complete a tax return, the next chapter is for you. That's where we dig deeper into data tracking and the tools available to help with that.

6. Tracking your data

Why collect data?

If tracking your data seems like yet another chore to add to a long list of things that need to be done but have nothing to do with improving text, please embrace it anyway. Why?

- It will save you time almost immediately.
- It will give you knowledge and confidence.
- It will help you frame pricing within a learning context rather than it being something that's dictated by others.

You can track your data however you wish but my recommendation is to use Microsoft Excel because it's already on most editors' desktops, and because it allows you to consolidate client and project data, invoicing and payment dates, and expenditure and tax obligations all in one place.

What to record and discover

The more data we record, the more clearly we're able to see how our pricing strategy impacts on individual projects *and* our overall business health, including information about the following:

- Average hourly and per-word rates
- Project start and end dates
- Fees – quotes, paid, pending and overdue
- Baselines data – word count, hours worked
- Project title, client, and how they found us
- The worth of each client as a percentage of total income
- Our most lucrative months
- Our most lucrative clients
- Our most lucrative projects
- Average editing speeds across different project types
- Year-on-year data comparisons
- Income to declare
- Allowable expenses to offset

Speed and more accurate estimation

Over time, we can accrue information that tells us how long a particular type of editing takes us on average, or whether Client A's work tends to be speedier to complete than Client B's. This helps us improve the quality of our minimum-required-rate calculations, and drives us towards our desired rates.

Client analysis

Some editors work for repeat clients – an agency or publisher, for example. In those cases, we're not always in control of the price, and yet those clients can still be valuable because of the amount of repeat work they send us and the percentage of our overall income their business accounts for.

Knowing who our most valuable clients are is essential if we're to avoid knee-jerk reactions to rates of pay when we're embracing a client-offer strategy.

If Publisher A pays us an hourly rate half that of Agency B but gives us five times as much work, we'll want to think carefully before canning that client on the grounds that their price is too low, or because a colleague said their pricing structure is 'unfair'.

Business mindset

Tracking reinforces a strategic mindset, one that shifts us away from negative and worrisome thoughts about how we might be 'doing pricing wrong' or letting the profession down.

Instead, we make decisions, input the data, review that data, and adjust our pricing based on the knowledge we've acquired about our particular business – not some rate-shaming discussion in a Facebook group.

I've looked upon my own data plenty of times over the years and discovered nuggets of information that I'd have been otherwise ignorant of:

- Client X's work was taking me longer than I'd budgeted for. I reviewed my pricing.
- Free sample edits were costing me a fortune in valuable time. I started charging.
- Client Y was more lucrative than I'd expected.

- Client Z, while not paying my standard current rate, still accounted for 13% of my income because of the volume of work they sent me.
- Australian editors buy a lot more books and courses from me than I'd anticipated.

Tools for the job

The spreadsheet template

Some editors have developed Excel templates that make taxation and business-health analysis a doddle. If you want something simple to get you going, help yourself to my freebie: Excel Scheduling Template.

If you want something amazing, invest in the skills of a pro who can customize your template with data that's relevant to you. One example is The Editor's Affairs from Maya Berger. Created for editors by an editor, it's an integrated system of Excel tools that keeps everything in one place. I use it and wouldn't be without it.

Keeping an eye on the clock

There are two desktop apps that stand out for independent editors who need to track time and want the option of monitoring projects for multiple clients in any one day, week or month.

- Toggl
- Clockify

They're free; they come with browser extensions so we can access them easily; and they offer simple on/off functionality when that's all we need.

Productivity tools

Make your pricing strategy work harder for you by integrating editing productivity tools into your working day. Examples include:

- Editing macros: Paul Beverley's editing macros are massive time-savers and completely free. There are hundreds to choose from and many come with complementary videos for new users.
- Microsoft Word's keyboard shortcuts function.
- Microsoft Word's onboard search and find/replace tools.

- Microsoft Word's onboard styles palette.
- Online dictionaries and style guides.
- PDF editing tools such as onboard comment/markup tools and bookmarks, and my proofreading stamps.
- PerfectIt: The ultimate consistency-checking and style-enforcing software. Another standout time-saving tool.
- TextExpander: Plugin that works across multiple platforms. Create keyboard shortcuts and generate longer custom oft-typed snippets. Great for emails, reports, signatures, and commenting in Word files.
- Report templates (fiction editors might be interested in my course which includes a ready-to-go template).

Summing up

Tracking our data helps us analyse our pricing. Using productivity tools helps us get more done in less time. If we're billing by the word or using a flat rate, we'll benefit. If we're billing by the hour, our clients will benefit. In that case, we might want to adjust our hourly rate, knowing the client won't pay more because we'll be more efficient.

7. Communicating the price

The different approaches

There are different ways of communicating a price to a client, either publicly or privately. Editors can mix and match if that suits them. This chapter reviews the five most common approaches:

- Per word
- Per hour
- Per page
- Flat rate
- Daily rate

Whichever option you choose, you'll still need data that tells you what you need to earn to at least break even.

Per word

Advantages

- The more efficient you are, the more profitable you are, assuming there are no surprises, and assuming you know your required rate.
- You're paid for your expertise, not your time.
- As you get better at your job, you become better off.
- Economies of scale kick in with longer projects.
- The client knows what the final price is even if the word count changes. More words means more money, and vice versa. It's therefore a good tool for price transparency.

Disadvantages

- If for whatever reason the work isn't going as planned – and the problem lies with you rather than the project – your inefficiency will affect your profitability. Of course, that's not a disadvantage for your client, and it could be argued that they shouldn't pay for your productivity problems anyway.

- Projects that turn out to be more complex than expected can eat into an editor's profitability. For example, Tim reviews a sample and quotes £15 per 1,000 words for copyediting. The file that ends up in his editing studio has multiple problems that he didn't budget for because they weren't evident from the sample. Now he's stuck with hours of additional work and no way to claw back the time unless he's prepared to have an awkward conversation with the client that in itself will take time.
- The maths can confuse those clients who don't put the decimal point in the right place when they convert from pence/cents to pounds/dollars. It's therefore sensible to give an example. E.g. 'I charge £20 per 1,000 words, meaning a file with 100,000 words will cost £2,000.' Or 'I charge 2 cents per word, meaning a file with 100,000 words will cost $2,000.'

Summary of editing fit

Consider per-word fees if:

- You work at sentence level and have informative historical data.
- You work at sentence level and are experienced, efficient and therefore faster.
- You price at the higher end, such that the payment for even unexpectedly complex jobs will exceed your required rate.
- You work on longer-form content.

Per hour

Advantages

- Time is valuable. Regardless of which pricing strategy an editor chooses, and how they convey their price, it's not unusual for the hourly rate to take centre stage when it comes to reviewing the health of a business. I charge on a per-word basis but my average hourly rate is a core metric that I reach for when I want to assess how profitable my business is.
- Shorter-form content comes with fewer economies of scale. An hourly rate doesn't penalize you for the time taken to get into the flow of a project.

- Time is a universal language and there's no maths involved. You're paid for the time you put in.
- Your inefficiencies are paid for by the client. The slower you are, the longer the job takes and the more the client pays. Some clients will therefore expect an estimation of how many hours a project will take; do alert the client if the estimation is likely to need adjustment.

Disadvantages

- Your efficiencies end up in the client's pocket rather than your own. The idea that experience and productivity become punitive disturbs a lot of editors, not least because it discourages improvement.
- Time is finite, which means as you get better at your job, you become worse off. Economies of scale work against you with longer projects.
- Even though there's no maths involved, uncertainty is in play. Unless you agree a ceiling on the number of hours a project will take, the client will be in the dark as to what the final bill will be. For price-sensitive clients especially, that could be an issue.
- Hourly rates encourage some editors to overly focus on the clock because the mindset from the get-go is framed around time rather than expertise.
- If the client wants a ceiling on the number of hours a job will take, less experienced editors might fall into the trap of overestimating their ability to deliver in a certain time frame so that they can price more competitively. When they're not as productive as they hoped, they end up less well off.

Summary of editing fit

Consider per-hour fees if:

- You work at sentence level but don't yet have a bank of historical data.
- You work at sentence level but are inexperienced and inefficient, and therefore slower.

- You work at structural/developmental level.
- You work on shorter-form content.

Per page

Advantages

- Assuming the client knows that a standard 'page' equates to 250 words, this approach has the same advantages as the per-word method – the more efficient you are, the more profitable you are.
- You're being paid for your expertise, not your time.
- Economies of scale kick in with longer-form content.
- More 'pages' mean more money, and vice versa.

Disadvantages

- Some clients have no clue that a standard publishing 'page' is 250 words. If you choose to quote in this way, make sure you explain the standard formula.
- Economies of scale are absent with shorter-form content.
- Some argue that working in pages adds unnecessary maths into the equation. If words convert to pages, why not just quote in the language of words?

Summary of editing fit

Consider per-page fees if:

- You're confident your clients understand what a publishing 'page' is.
- You're experienced and efficient, and want to be paid for your expertise, not your efficiency.
- You work at sentence level.
- You work on longer-form content.

Flat rate

Advantages

- The more efficient you are, the more profitable you are, assuming there are no surprises, and assuming you know your required rate.
- You're paid for your expertise, not your time.
- As you get better at your job, you become better off.
- Economies of scale kick in with longer projects.
- Projects for regular clients are easier to estimate accurately because you're familiar with their requirements.
- It's transparent. The client knows what the final project price will be regardless of the word count or any hiccups during the editing process.
- The fee is tailored to the project rather than the number of words.

Disadvantages

- Complex projects, and those for new clients, can be difficult to estimate without historical data.
- Editors must have a precise understanding of the scope of the project. Time for evaluation therefore needs to be factored into the fee.
- If the editor can't assess a complex project in its entirety before quoting, the risk of underestimating increases.
- There are lower economies of scale with shorter projects. Editors need to factor this in to their calculation.

Summary of editing fit

Consider a flat rate if:

- You have experience of evaluating a project.
- You have historical data to guide you.
- You work with repeat clients.

- You are comfortable offering differential flat fees that acknowledge economies of scale.
- You work on complex projects that need a custom approach.

Daily rate

Advantages

- Assuming the project's scope is clearly understood, you're rewarded for efficiency and experience.
- If the client is unable to clarify what they want but requires editorial expertise on hand (and perhaps on site), the editor receives a fixed fee for a day's work regardless of the outcome.
- You and the client both know up front what's required, how long you will be available for, and what the cost will be.

Disadvantages

- Less experienced editors with no historical data, or who are working for new clients, will struggle to estimate what can be achieved in a day.
- You're tied down to one client, which precludes you from slotting in shorter pieces of work.
- If the work turns out to be more complex than you expected, and extends beyond the agreed number of days, the client might not be prepared to pay more.

Summary of editing fit

Consider a daily rate if:

- You're asked to work on site or be on hand at a given time.
- The client is more focused on your availability than what you cost.
- You have experience of evaluating a project and historical data to guide you.
- You like structure.

Summing up

When deciding how to communicate a rate, consider the type of editing you're doing, how familiar you are with the client's writing, how experienced and efficient you are, the project's word count, the project's scope, and the extent to which historical data can guide you. There's no single best fit for every editor or every project, so mix and match as required.

8. Build a quote that converts

Getting the message right

This chapter is not about how to build a quote from scratch. The Chartered Institute of Editing and Proofreading's *Pricing a Project: How to Prepare a Professional Quotation* by Melanie Thompson already does an outstanding job of digging into the nitty-gritty of quotations for even complex editing projects.

What we're focusing on here is how to get the messaging right so that quoting becomes more than just about a price for a job. Instead, it's a marketing and branding tool that demonstrates editorial excellence and works on the client's emotions.

Compelling quotations work especially well for editors with a value-based pricing strategy because they likely have existing resources they can use to make their quote stand out.

Why quoting is part of marketing and branding

If we've made ourselves visible enough to be asked to quote, that quotation needs to sparkle with value. A poor response is just poor marketing and branding.

We're not alone

It's never been easier or quicker to find an editor and get a quotation. That's great news because any one of us can make ourselves visible. That's just the first step, though, because the client has probably asked more than one editor to quote. And so they should have. They're trying to find the best-fit editor – someone with the right skills, experience, availability, fee structure, and personality for them. And just because we've made the final three, five, ten (or whatever) doesn't mean any of us will get the gig. If none of us floats the client's boat, they'll head back to the search engines and directories in a jiffy. There are plenty more editing fish in the sea.

We must never forget the competition when we're quoting. We're not alone; we're one among thousands. Standing out is essential.

Is the author really just asking for a quote?

Most of us have been interviewed at some time. Questions are asked and we respond. But we're not assessed on just the words that come out of our mouths. The interviewer(s) will also be influenced (sometimes unintentionally) by how we smile; what we're wearing; whether we seem friendly, confident and engaged; whether we arrive in a timely manner; and the degree to which the answers we deliver reflect the CV we submitted.

It's the same when we respond to quotation requests. Our authors, too, will be influenced by the engagement we show, the speed of our response, the tone we use, and whether that matches what they were expecting. Imagine you and I have just sat down in a restaurant. You ask me what my favourite chocolate is. My response is one of the following:

1. 'Lindt.'
2. 'I absolutely love Lindt. It's delicious. Just thinking about it brings to mind Christmas when I was a kid.'
3. 'Lindt. That company sources high-quality beans from sustainable cocoa-farming programmes. And it tastes divine.'

If all you want to know is what my favourite chocolate is, then (1) answers the question. But if we're chatting over dinner, I'm not exactly helping the conversation along. You might think me rather dull. You might be texting Uber. You might already have your coat on. The other two responses tell you something more about me. Answer (2) might evoke a sense of warmth and openness. Answer (3) might evoke a sense of my political and environmental values. Either way, both show that I'm interested in your question, that I'm prepared to give thought to it.

Our responses to requests to quote need to demonstrate engagement and thoughtfulness too. Getting a cab with Uber is quick. Deleting an email is quicker.

We might be able to change their mind

Perhaps the author's done their editor search with the intention of sourcing three hundred pounds' worth of proofreading within the next month. Based on the sample, we think it needs seven hundred pounds' worth of copyediting. Plus, we have a wait list of six months.

We don't know what the author's budget is but that's not what matters. What matters is that they do, and it's way lower than what's in the email we've just sent them. And the time frame is just wrong.

When we add value – and we'll talk below about ways to do that – we might be able to change their mind. Maybe they'll say:

> 'I'd planned to have this turned around within the next few weeks, but you've blown me away. You're worth waiting for.'

Or:

> 'I'll be honest – that's a lot more than I'd budgeted for. However, you've really nailed what I'm struggling with, and I think you're worth it.'

Or they might become our champion

Sometimes we won't be able to change the author's mind because the budget or the timing just isn't right. But that doesn't mean we won't stay top of mind. Perhaps they'll say:

> 'I really, really need to get this out now, so I'm going to walk away. But I want you to know that I would have loved you to edit my book. Here's a testimonial.'

Or:

> 'I'm really sad that I can't afford you. You're worth every penny. Next time I'll plan ahead and save up.'

And even though they haven't hired us, they'll still be our champion. Perhaps they'll tell another writer about us, or maybe they will plan ahead with the next book and save up for us. When we add value, we're not just quoting for this job, we're quoting for future jobs too.

People who don't know us

When we're contacted by someone who's never met us before, trust issues are already in play. For the less experienced author, sourcing editing can feel like a high-risk venture. Unlike for doctors or electricians, there's nothing to stop anyone entering professional practice. Editors can't be struck off.

Here's what an author recently told me:

> 'My problem is one that's all too common across all aspects of the indie publishing landscape. The barriers to entry are few (a website) and the options available to a customer to confirm or verify quality are limited and poor, short of taking a test drive.'

We need to help potential clients confirm or verify quality. Adding value is part of that process.

Our brand is at stake

Responses to quotation requests need to be on-brand. Branding is not just about having an eye-catching logo. It's about conveying the essence of what we stand for at every touchpoint of our business – from our website and business cards to our emails and invoices.

There's little point in having a compelling website if our quotation responses are forgettable or off-putting.

Whether our passion lies in editing for students, academics, corporates, or novelists, our quotations need to reflect that passion. Offering value – something beyond 'This is what it will cost and when I can do it' – is one way of reinforcing that brand identity and moving away from an any-old-editor mentality.

How to add value to the quote

Include a digital swag bag of relevant hero resources

Let's imagine your evaluation of the sample indicates problems with dialogue tagging and viewpoint. What if, in addition to telling the author your price and availability, you gave them two free booklets that offer guidance on how they might rectify those problems in the book you're quoting for or in their future writing.

Even if those booklets are on your website, don't assume the author has downloaded them. Maybe they didn't get round to it, or perhaps they found you through a different platform.

Hero content adds value in multiple ways:

- It demonstrates engagement and thoughtfulness – we're showing we understand what the client's problems are, and are providing solutions.
- It offers proof of expertise – we have the knowledge, and that helps to build trust.
- It stands out – most editors don't offer free booklets or free resources.

Do a mini sample edit

Even if we usually charge for sample line/copyedits or proofreads of a thousand or so words, we might do a mini one for free – a couple of hundred words. This delivers value in the form of the following:

- Engagement and thoughtfulness – you're giving the author something valuable that they can measure or use for comparative purposes.
- Expertise – you're demonstrating your abilities; showing the difference it would make if the client were to choose you.
- Acknowledgement of subjectivity – you're helping the author assess whether your style of editing fits their expectations.

Provide a teeny critique

Another option is to offer a short critique of the sample they've sent. I'm not suggesting a five-page report, but rather a few paragraphs that summarize the main problems as you see them, illustrated with a few examples.

As with the free mini sample edit, it's something they can use, and it demonstrates our knowledge of and engagement with their craft.

This is an opportunity to show not only how we'd get under the skin of the writing, but also how working with us would push the author's project forward.

Be a little personal

How about including a personal snippet that responds to something in their enquiry that truly resonated with you?

- Perhaps they mentioned being inspired by a love of a particular author's published works. If you're a fan, too, tell them.
- Maybe they told you this is their first attempt at business writing. If you're an editor who's written business materials, tell them so, and include a few words to show that you understand what it's like to start out on the writing journey.
- Did something about the premise of their scientific journal article really stand out for you in the sample? Maybe you know someone else who works in this field, or their research reminds you of a related article that you worked on in the past and found fascinating.
- If they've expressed concerns about anything – fear of being edited, confidentiality, new-author nerves, then express your empathy and address those issues with solutions.

Whatever you choose to communicate, remember that it's a small personal connector that says, 'I get you.' It shows that something about the author or their project excites you, and reflects your desire to invest in the project. When we feel that itch, we're starting on a journey too, one that compels us to do a standout job. Communicating this in some small way can help us to earn the author's trust.

Show enthusiasm

We must remember to ensure that the tone of our message conveys a desire to do the job. 'This is what it will cost and when I can do it' won't inspire confidence in any author who's even slightly nervous about working with an editor … not on its own.

If, like me, you love your job, and think it's a privilege to get paid for doing something you enjoy, use language that conveys that passion. Tell your potential clients that you *want* to work with them, that you'd relish the chance help them with their writing journey.

Talk to them about the price and your availability, of course. That's what was asked for and it must be front and centre. But that's only where we start because when it comes to the fee we're offering, it's not enough to think, *I'm worth that*. Worth has to be proved.

Framing quotes in terms of what the author saves

Recall the tiered pricing strategy I mentioned in Chapter 2. Here's an excerpt from an email I received in 2020 from a client who'd agreed to pay £75 for a sample edit of 1,000 words.

> 'Before I pay for the 1,000-word sample edit, I have a question. Would you offer a discount if you were to edit the whole short story of 5,500 words or would it be 5½ times £75?'

This email showed me how I'd made a mistake in not trying to upgrade the project at an earlier stage by framing it in terms of what the author could save. Notice how they're thinking in terms of discount. They're not quibbling about my rates but they *are* thinking about their budget, as they should. I replied that I did indeed offer reduced rates for larger word counts and offered a price of £299.75 for the short story. The author leapt at the chance because they saw an opportunity to save money.

I also told them what I'd have charged if the story had been 80,000 words, in the hope that if they have a novel in them, they'll come back to me for a bigger saving in future.

It's a good reminder that we must try to put ourselves in our clients' shoes when we're quoting rather than making assumptions. If they've already raised their hand and expressed an interest in our services, reframing our rates in terms of what they could save rather than what they are spending could convert a small project into a larger one with a higher total price tag.

Summing up

In a noisy, global online market, creating compelling quotes takes effort. If that effort helps us secure the opportunities to work for our ideal clients, it'll be time well spent. An editor with no work is not running a business; they're unemployed. Every minute we spend adding value to our quotations is an investment in employment and business ownership.

9. Going public with pricing

Transparency or privacy?

Some editors choose to be transparent about their rates; others consider their fees proprietorial. Both approaches have advantages and disadvantages.

It's worth testing both approaches to see which works best for you and your business. Since it's the more visible (and emotive) option, we'll look here at the advantages and disadvantages of transparency. The inverse is true in each case for privacy regarding rates (e.g. if an advantage of transparency is that it filters out clients who can't afford us, the disadvantage of privacy is that clients might be reluctant to contact us because they have no idea of how much we might charge).

Advantages

Filtering out clients who can't afford us

Some clients who land on our websites or find us in directories are the perfect fit in terms of project, time frame, and attitude towards the value of editing. Nevertheless, they can't afford us. It's not about disrespect or price-shopping. Rather, the numbers don't add up. Perhaps they've set aside £800 for proofreading but our rate card indicates a price of £1,200 for their project. They won't budge. Nor will we. Pricing transparency means we don't waste each other's time, lovely though it would have been to work together.

Deterring or attracting price-shoppers

Some clients are looking for the cheapest deal they can get. That doesn't make them bad people. Rather, they have different priorities in relation to how they spend their money. Many will be aware that some highly qualified professional editors compete on price. If you're one of those editors (and it's perfectly okay if you are), transparent pricing will give you an advantage over higher-priced editors. If you're one of the higher-priced editors, transparent pricing will deter the price-shoppers, meaning you and the price-shopping client don't waste each other's time.

Brand signalling

If honesty, integrity and openness are part of your brand, there's an argument that price transparency feeds into this, regardless of whether you're pricing at the lower or higher end. Making our prices public is one way of *showing* these brand signals rather than telling them.

Being public with prices also tells the market clearly what *we* think we're worth regardless of whether someone else thinks we're cheap or expensive.

Bear in mind that this could work against you with a penetration or discount pricing strategy. Premium rates might be *perceived* as indicating higher quality, while budget rates could indicate a lower-quality service and desperation. Publicizing penetration and discount prices is therefore best done in campaign form rather than on rate cards. That way, permanency won't be attached to the pricing structure.

Matching buyer expectations

Few of us could imagine buying a television, washing machine, car, holiday or train ticket without seeing the price before we contact the seller. There's a strong argument that the same applies to editorial services.

Making room for negotiation

Negotiations rarely move up from a baseline. If you're not competing on price and you've set your fees at what most editors would deem to be the higher end, but you're prepared to negotiate, a public price puts you in a position where you can move down without damaging profitability.

Disadvantages

Client confusion

Perhaps you work with clients with differing price sensitivities (e.g. multinationals, government departments and charities). In that case, your prices might be so varied that presenting a pricing structure on a rate card is impossible.

Or perhaps you have clients with similar price sensitivities but the level of intervention required is so variable that even a range would be so wide as to be nonsensical (e.g. copyediting for independent novelists).

Leaving no room for negotiation

If you're competing on price and have set your fees at what most editors would deem to be the lower end, a public price puts you in a position where you might have nowhere to go that isn't unprofitable.

Poor anchoring that deters good-fit clients

If being public with prices tells the market what *we* think we're worth, transparency can work against us if there are no other signals to anchor our pricing decisions. An editor whose prices are considered high but who offers little to justify their worth in the form of standout added value might cause a client to evaluate them on price only.

Public pricing works best at the higher end when the value of an editor's content mirrors the price on display. If you're going public, a vibrant blog, a suite of free checklists and templates, an outstanding portfolio, excellent testimonials, or a channel of how-to video tutorials is valuable content that will anchor your prices. When good-fit clients think they can't afford you, great content encourages them to negotiate.

Rate-shaming

Unfortunately, rates discussions in editorial forums too frequently end up with someone being told that their rates are an insult, that they impact negatively on the professional status of editors, and that they drive a 'race to the bottom' in which clients expect to get a lot and pay a little. I believe this is nonsense. You might have a different opinion. However, if you're a new entrant whose rates are relatively low and you're thinking about pricing transparency, you should be aware of possible kickback from some quarters.

Either take no notice or remind the shamer that none of us needs to justify our pricing strategies. Nor does anyone have the right to shame another for charging more or less than them; they don't know enough about the other's circumstances to make informed assessments.

And remember these wise words from fiction editor Crystal Watanabe: 'There's an editor for every budget.' Or these from non-fiction editor Denise Cowle's Great Auntie Margaret: 'Every teacup has a saucer.' So it does.

How to make your prices public

Rate cards

I recommend the following:

- Focus on the core information.
- Design it so that it's on-brand and looks like any other content from your stable.
- Track downloads so you know whether it's getting traction.
- Don't forget to include your web address.

At the time of writing, Google Analytics doesn't show us which content from our websites has been downloaded. StatCounter does. An alternative is to 'gate' your rate card by asking someone to sign up for it (via MailChimp, for example). If that doesn't appeal, create a pricing page on your website.

Website widgets and plugins

Include a calculation tool on your website that gives a client a ballpark figure. Two widgets on offer are:

- Calconic
- ConvertCalculator

Pricing page on your website

This can be a web-page version of your rate card. Don't forget to include a call-to-action button. These have been proved to drive clients to do what you want them to do.

A not-so-public alternative: The fast ballpark price

Ballpark pricing is that which gives the client an initial and fast indication of what a project might cost. There's no project evaluation involved, which means the editor's working with numbers based on average speeds, and the client's working with word counts or some other given element – for example, a web page of up to X words; a publishing 'page' of 250 words; X hours of the editor's time, and so on.

Of course, we can provide ballparks on rate cards, on web pages, and via online instant-quote widgets if we want to go public. However, an alternative is a halfway house whereby we offer **a fast ballpark quote** via email or phone. This might appeal to the editor who doesn't want to go public, but who does want to deter poor-fit clients fast.

Filtering with the ballpark

Some years ago, I arranged for a sales rep to visit with a view to securing a quote for some new windows to be fitted. I took the rep around our house and showed him which windows needed replacing. Then I sat through a 45-minute pitch about the company and the quality of its products. I was frustrated after five minutes and couldn't wait to get the guy out of the door. While quality is important, and the fine detail might have been useful later, I didn't want to spend my valuable time listening to someone selling a product to me that ultimately I couldn't afford. I wanted a ballpark price first.

Many of our clients are no different. If an independent author has a figure of £400 in her head for an 83,000-word proofread, and my ballpark quotation is £500, we'll probably continue the discussion because the gap between what they want to pay and what I want to charge is bridgeable. If my ballpark quotation is around the £1,500 mark, it's a different story. That's nearly quadruple what the client hoped for. I'm certainly not going to come down by 70%, and I doubt they'll go up by 375%.

My rates are calculated by estimating the time it will take to complete an editing project and pricing that time in such a way that I earn what I want and need in order to make my business sustainable. My client's preferred price is based on ... actually, I have no idea what it's based on. And it doesn't matter what it's based on. All that matters is that neither of us has wasted each other's time having a lengthy email discussion about the value I bring to the table set against the financial pressures they're under when, in fact, we're just not a good financial fit for each other at this point in time.

Our time has a cost to it. Our clients' time has a cost to it, too. The ballpark figure – just like the public price – allows both parties to move on quickly and spend our time in ways that are more appropriate to each of us, but because the client has made direct contact, we still have an opportunity to add value at the fast-quote stage should we wish to (see Chapter 8).

Engaging with the client

Some customers simply want to know the price quickly. It's not that they're trying to get our services on the cheap, or that they don't value what we do for them. Rather, they want to be able to plan their budget as quickly as possible.

Consider, again, the author mentioned above. They have an 83,000-word novel that needs proofreading. They have no idea what proofreaders charge, but they do want to hire one and are prepared to find the funds necessary to secure the services of an editor who instils confidence in them. They've looked online and found a few whose websites they liked and who made them feel like they'd be in safe hands. To some extent, the value those proofreaders will bring to the project has already been acknowledged. At this stage, they want to get a feel for what their investment will likely be – will they need to save up or do they already have the funds in place? Acquiring a ballpark figure prior to having a lengthier discussion about the proofreading process will help get the ball rolling.

In some cases, the ballpark price enables us to engage with the client and nail the deal before they've had a chance to search elsewhere.

What a ballpark isn't

Ballpark prices should be as realistic as possible. It's not a trick price to lure a client into a conversation, only for us to turn around and say, 'Sorry, it's going to be double the fee I quoted earlier.' Rather, it's meant to facilitate a conversation that enables us to cut to the chase and decide as quickly as possible whether we're a financial fit. There will be times, of course, when the ballpark and confirmed quotations are far apart because, following an assessment of the project, the level of intervention required is either beyond our skill set or requires more time. Hitting the mark comes with experience and data (see Chapter 6).

For editors who work on highly complex projects, offering a realistic price without seeing at least a sample of the work and discussing the project's parameters will be impossible, even foolhardy.

Does the ballpark focus on money over value?

The argument goes that ballpark quotes focus on the money rather than the value that editorial professionals bring to the table. When we offer ballpark quotes, it's just a figure. Says Celine Roque:

> 'It's incomplete. Your quote is just a number. Your clients can't surmise all the information they need from that number. Apart from the primary services you provide, you

should also give them your advice. Oftentimes, what a client really needs is different from what they think they need. In this case, an assessment of a client's business and project, followed by a proposal, is the better approach.'

The problem is that giving advice takes time. Furthermore, what a client *needs* is not always the same thing as what a client *wants*. Giving advice to someone who actually just wants a price isn't good customer service (even if we know that our advice, value, etc. would, in reality, be in their best interests). It's just aggravating. There are ways to give advice that aren't invasive:

- We can give our advice later, once we've provided what the client asked for – the price.
- We can offer that advice in other places on our website, e.g. via blogs, booklets, videos and fact sheets.
- We can link to those resources in the fast quote.

Do ballparks shut the door to negotiation?

Steve Payne of the Sexton Group says of his 'number one rule of quoting prices':

> 'Don't quote a price – any price – before you have sold the client on your ability to do the job. If you haven't convinced the client that it's you they want to work with, before you quote a price, it's like you are swinging at a baseball too early. In the case above, you made no effort to tell the client, through testimonials, through photographs, through stories, about your firm. How it operates. What makes it different. How delighted past customers have been with your work. How you have many repeat clients who will never work with another contractor as long as you are in business.'

In other words, you're potentially shutting the door to negotiation, especially if your price is perceived as too high. Payne's point about using value to make you a more hireable prospect is excellent, but I still believe that when a potential client asks for a price, we need to listen to that request and act on it. No one wants to hire an editor who can't follow a brief. If we can't listen to a client's request at the very first point of contact, how can we expect them to trust us to listen further down the line?

To ameliorate this, consider other ways in which you can emphasize your value at the point where clients are likely to contact you.

- Put testimonials on every page of your website, including your contact page (and pricing page if you go down this route).
- Offer useful tools and resources for your ideal clients – content that *shows* rather than tells your worth.
- Make your website about client solutions.
- Build a portfolio and make sure it's accessible. It's a powerful form of social proof.

Overcoming anxiety about public prices

If you're nervous about price transparency, consider these options:

- Offer a **price range** instead of single numbers.
- Consider the **impact on leads against profits**. You might be better off even though you're receiving fewer leads.
- Think about whether you're **filtering** out clients that you wouldn't have wanted to work for anyway.
- If you're concerned about deterring particular groups of clients for whom you'd reduce your advertised price, indicate that you're happy to have discussions about **custom pricing arrangements** (e.g. with charities or not-for-profits).
- Public pricing statements are generally considered to be top-end discussion starters. Having one won't necessarily stop someone from getting in touch; it won't stop them **negotiating** either.
- Wait until you have a **buffer** – several bookings lined up a few months ahead – then test public pricing for a month. Keep an eye on downloads or views, and the effect on queries and your book of work.
- If, after trialling, you believe the impact of public pricing is detrimental to your business, **tweak and retest** or **ditch** it. Either way, you learned something valuable.
- Consider **multiple public price points**, each of which talks to different client types. Lots of other businesses do this – social media management tools, for example.

Case study – the emotionality of pricing

Time to put my money where my mouth is.

In my heart, I'm committed to transparency. But my head tells me I need data. And so I've tested public pricing three times during my freelance career, and each time I've reverted to privacy – talking money only *after* direct contact has been made by the potential client.

That doesn't mean public pricing is the wrong decision for you. My choice is particular to me and my business. The reason I offer this case study is because my decisions are informed by experience, and because that experience has led me to consider further the emotionality of pricing.

My most recent transparency venture occurred in June 2020. I uploaded a branded rate card to my website and waited to see what would happen.

During the pandemic, only one client cancelled, and I was given several months' notice. My editing schedule was therefore stable. And while I noticed a minor drop-off in requests for quotes during the very early stages of UK lockdown, at no stage did things come to a standstill. I can't say the same for my experiment with a rate card.

I left my rate card up for a month, then pulled it. Things returned to normal; authors began to get in touch regularly.

Observations

Not having public prices on my website might well deter some authors from getting in touch, but it doesn't deter enough to make it a problem. I therefore don't believe private pricing damages my business.

Having a public rate card *does* appear to deter authors from making contact. Over the course of my 2020 month-long test, only one author contacted me for a quote, and accepted my price, and that was on day 2. After that, the silence was deafening. I therefore believe public pricing damages my business.

I don't believe my prices are the problem. If they were, I wouldn't be able to convert email or phone requests to quote into confirmed bookings priced identically to the fees advertised on my rate card. Something else must be in play.

Emotional hurdling

I'm an example of an editor who invests time in creating a lot of useful problem-solving content that I believe compels ideal clients to get in touch because I've shown them I know my stuff and am engaged with their journey. That strategy works when my pricing is private – enough clients will pay the fee I want to earn. When I go public, it's not enough. Here's what I think is going on.

I suspect the rate card is pulling them out of their emotional decision-making mindset and focusing them on impersonal numbers. There's a big difference between downloading a pretty PDF that says: *Line editing: £X per 1,000 words* and a personal email that thanks the author for taking the time to get in touch, iterates my enjoyment of reading the sample, lists some strengths and weaknesses I've identified, links to some useful resources, offers line editing at £X per 1,000 words, and wishes them a good weekend.

The language of the rate card is numerical. The language of the email is emotional. The phrasing I employ will include personal pronouns. For example:

- 'Thank *you* for sending the sample'
- '*I* would love to line edit *your* novel for *you*'
- '*I*'d like to offer *you* a price of £X per 1,000 words'
- 'if *we* can agree terms'
- '*I* can begin editing *your* book on this date if that works for *you*'

It's the cordial language of a team, of a journey, of consensus-seeking.

I believe my web-based rate card is talking money too soon. It's a distraction from all the emotional nudging I've done. The author's already online – it's not hard for them to click back to Google or return to the directory they found me in and search for someone else, just in case. In contrast, if we're having a discussion about pricing via email, it's because they've already made a jump based on that emotional nudging – one that's about saying hello and having a conversation.

Imagine an Olympic hurdler who's ahead of everyone else on the track. A TV presenter from a sports channel wants to interview them. That's not going to happen if the athlete hasn't jumped the last hurdle. First, they need to finish the race and take a breather. Only then can the conversation start. Maybe it's not so different for me and my clients. The rate card is coming before the final hurdle.

Summing up

Even if public pricing unnerves you, think about what it might look like if you tried it. How might you approach it in a way that sits comfortably with your client base and your brand? Then consider at least testing it. That way your decision to continue, tweak or ditch will be based on knowledge rather than fear. If like me, you decide to stay private, that's fine. Go your own way.

10. Strategies for increasing prices

This chapter offers several approaches to increasing editing prices and declining lower-paid work. These respect editors' differing circumstances, client bases, and preferences.

Reviewing our prices on a regular basis is good business practice because our income needs to keep up with cost-of-living increases and our business goals.

How strong is our position?

If we have a range of client types, raising our prices might not be straightforward:

- If we're price-acceptors, the fee model will be client-offer. In other words, a publisher, packager or agency decides the rate for the job.
- If we're price-setters, our strategy will be one of the other options discussed earlier in the guide. In this case, we decide what an independent author, student or business will pay.

Regardless of which strategy we choose and whether we're acceptors or setters, we're always in a position to raise our prices. What we *don't* have control over is whether our clients will pay. You or I might think our revised required or desired fee is entirely justified, but that's irrelevant:

- When we're price-acceptors, our clients are within their rights to maintain their current fees (or even decrease them), while we're within our rights to negotiate, or decline the work and walk away.
- When we're price-setters, we're within our rights to increase our fees. On the flip side, our clients are within their rights to decline the new price and walk away.

Thus, any change to a pricing model must consider the client's potential response and be carefully planned.

Avoiding knee-jerk thinking

If a colleague says they've decided to no longer edit for 'low' rates or announces that they're doubling their rates, we can congratulate them on their business decision. What we mustn't do is assume that the same decision is right for us.

- What do they mean by 'low' rates? Is our definition of 'low' the same as theirs? We might think £25 an hour for editing is great but a colleague may think it's unacceptable.
- What does 'doubling' mean? If colleague A increases their prices from £5 an hour to £10 an hour, they'll double their income. Great, but that's of little use to us if our required rate is £30 per hour. And if we're already charging £30 per hour, would our existing client base tolerate £60 per hour, or would we have to find new clients who'd pay that price?
- Do they have a supporting income that enables them to implement their decision immediately with no harm to their lifestyle? Perhaps their partner is the primary breadwinner, or they have an independent income. A colleague who can afford to immediately decline £25 per hour on principle is in a different position to us if we're responsible for all our monthly outgoings and can't risk earning zero pounds per hour until we've acquired a replacement client.
- Do they have a large and established client base in a sector that's known to be less price-sensitive than the sectors we work in? Perhaps their knowledge and specialist skills enable them to name their price. We, on the other hand, might work in a more competitive generalist market where we're easy to replace.
- Is their visibility so high that they're confident they can replace lost clients with new ones who'll pay their desired prices? Their marketing strategy might be mature, whereas we're still building our visibility and juggling feast and famine.

We must not feel compelled to increase prices or decline work just because our colleagues deem that what's on offer is a bum deal. Their current circumstances might be different from ours. Not everyone can afford to be unemployed, and the choices available to the owner of a mature freelance business might be different from those on offer to the beginner.

Strategy choices: The price-acceptor

When we're price-acceptors, the options are as follows:

Strategy 1: Flat refusal

The client offers work at a price we deem too low. We decline and walk away. Either we've acquired a better-paying replacement or we now have a gap in our schedule and are earning less.

Strategy 2: Negotiation

The client offers work at a price we deem too low. We negotiate. The outcome could be the rate we want, a rate that's in the middle ground and that will do until we have alternative work lined up, or a no-budge. If we get the rate we want, great. If we end up in the middle ground or with a no-budge, we must decide whether to walk away or move to phase-out mode.

Strategy 3: Phase out

The client offers work at a price we deem too low. We accept the fee but commit to find a better-paying replacement, at which point we phase out this customer.

Case study

In the early years of owning my editorial business, I was almost exclusively a price-acceptor. My main clients were publishers and packagers. I didn't think in terms of 'low' and 'high'. I thought in terms of experience, testimonials and portfolio generation, all of which I believed would make me more interesting and discoverable further down the line. Price comparisons were interesting but nothing more. They didn't determine whether I accepted or declined work.

I was completely replaceable in the eyes of my publisher and packager clients. They knew exactly where to go to find equally experienced editorial pros if I declined to work for them.

My marketing was ongoing, but I wasn't so visible that I could decline work from a publisher, safe in the knowledge that the gap in my schedule would be filled with a better-paying client. Saying no meant risking earning zero pounds per hour. Given that my income was important to our household, I took a cautious approach.

During that phase, I employed **negotiation** and **phasing-out strategies**. I took on work that gave me a full schedule. I gained experience and testimonials, and expanded my portfolio – all great marketing tools. As I acquired better-paying clients, I phased out the lower-paying ones.

Now my marketing strategy has paid off. I'm interesting and discoverable enough that I can decline a price and walk away. I've moved from negotiation and phasing-out to responding with a **flat refusal**.

Strategy choices: The price-setter

When we're price-setters, the options are as follows:

Strategy 1: Flat increase

We offer the client a price. If they accept, we do the work. If they decline, we walk. We're confident we can fill the gap in our schedule, but if we can't it doesn't matter because of our particular financial circumstances.

Strategy 2: Negotiation

We offer the client a price. The client wants to work with us but tries to bring the fee down. If we need to fill the space in our schedule and aren't confident that we'll acquire a replacement, we'll negotiate. The outcome could be a rate we're still more than happy with, a rate that's in the middle ground and that will do until we have alternative work lined up, or a no-budge. If we get the rate we want, great. If we end up in the middle ground or with a no-budge, we'll decide whether to walk away or buckle.

Strategy 3: Phase in

This is a good approach for established clients. The price increase is staggered so that the client has time to adjust. It can be presented as an extended discount that respects the pre-existing relationship. The client views it as valuable because they're getting a special benefit.

Case study

In the early years of owning my editorial business, I had few clients for whom I set the price, and I was still developing my visibility. If there was space in my schedule, I'd try to fill it by **negotiating** and **phasing in** price increases for regular clients.

Now things have changed. I'm a **flat-increaser** with new clients. If the client doesn't like the fee on offer, no problem. I thank them for their interest and wish them luck.

The replaceability issue is more complex now. New indie author enquirers can easily get comparative quotes so I'm operating in a competitive environment, but my branding is built around driving emotional decisions and deterring price-shopping clients.

With repeat indie clients, there's an existing relationship based on trust, and satisfaction with my previous work. I wouldn't go as far as to say I'm irreplaceable, but I have a value-based advantage when it comes to discussing increased prices and **phase in** price increases.

I'm also visible and have a long wait list. If my set price isn't acceptable to a new lead, I can walk away, confident that the slot in my schedule will be filled and that there's time for the right-fit client to find me.

Key factors

As the two case studies demonstrate, the price-increase strategies we choose can vary over time and depend on individual circumstances. There's no one-size-fits-all response. Here are some other factors to consider when increasing prices.

Consider the impact on income

A flat-refusal or a flat-increase strategy might have unpalatable consequences. What will be the impact on your income if you or the client walk away? Can you afford it? If not, a gentler transition will be in order – one that includes negotiation, phasing in or out, and taking a longer-term view of your business goals.

Plan ahead

Price increases should be founded on a plan for how to replace what we might lose. I prefer to assume the worst – that if I increase the rate there's a very real chance the client will walk. Being pessimistic means preparing ourselves well ahead of time with regular marketing that puts us top of mind (or top of Google) for the types of client who'll pay what we want to earn. After all, we must be visible to those clients who won't quibble over the price we want to charge or be offered.

Analyse the data

Flat refusals and flat increases should be based on realistic assessments of the potential financial loss rather than on impulsive reactions to feeling undervalued.

For some of us, at certain stages of our careers, it's better to be underpaid and overwhelmed with work than overpaid but underwhelmed. We all want to be overpaid and overwhelmed but that doesn't happen just because we decide that's what we want!

Be realistic

Don't underestimate your value, but don't overestimate it either. Even if you think you put the *oo* into proofreader, your client might decide they can afford to lose you. That's not to say you should buckle. Rather, you need to have a plan B – a replacement client.

Don't be a sheep

We're independent business owners. Ultimately, we need to work out what to charge, what to accept, when to say yes or no, who to work for and how to be found.

Colleagues' calls for us to double our rates, decline work, and increase our prices this way or that way are based on little to no information about *our* circumstances. For that reason, just as they cannot be the primary determiners of *what* we charge, they cannot be the primary determiners of *how* we increase our prices.

Don't take it personally

If we lose a client because we can't find a mutually acceptable price point, it's not a slur on our character or our abilities. It's just business. We have to look after ours, and our clients have to look after theirs. Sometimes a fit just can't be found.

Summing up

Whether we buckle, negotiate, phase in/out, or make flat-out decisions, our price increases should be based on our circumstances. There's no strategy that's right or wrong, and no shame in which choice we make as long as it's done in relation to an analysis of our business needs and goals.

11. Why the 'race to the bottom' argument is flawed

Those who choose to enter the editing market with short-term penetration- or discount-pricing strategies, or try to make sense of competitors' prices, or come up with cost-based, customer-based, or democratic prices, can fall foul of rate-shaming when their price is public and other editors think it's too low.

We've already looked at why other people's subjective opinions of our rates don't help us make decisions informed by our needs and preferences. In this chapter, we'll look at why the premise behind the 'race to the bottom' argument is flawed.

Competing with cheap

I live in Norwich, UK. In the city centre, there's a mall with a discount store selling techie stuff – phones, tablets and whatnot. People go into that shop expecting a deal, which means they're price-shopping. It's not that they're terrible people who are always looking for cheap. Rather, the coffers are low. Maybe the car failed its MOT and they had to find an extra seven hundred quid that month. Perhaps they recently lost their job. Perhaps they're paying for private tuition for a child with particular educational needs. That store's pricing strategy is likely a cost-based, customer-based, and discount-based hybrid. Some might even argue that it's a democratic strategy.

On the floor above is an Apple store selling shiny things for shiny people. No one enters that store expecting a deal. They enter expecting to pay what they have to pay to get the shiny thing they want. It's where people go when they're product- or service-shopping. The coffers are flush. The car passed its MOT, the job is secure, and their child is in mainstream schooling paid for by the state. Apple's pricing strategy is value-based.

All clients are not the same

Apple could decide not to have a store in that mall. It could say, 'This is ridiculous. No one's going to buy our stuff when they can get similar products from the store on the floor below for one fifth of the price. That discount store is encouraging a race to the bottom.'

But Apple doesn't say that. Why? Because it knows that the customers who come into the mall aren't all the same. Some won't come near the Apple store because the prices are too high. But others – those who are looking specifically for an Apple product, those who are Apple fans, those whose attachment to the Apple brand is emotional, those whose cars passed their MOTs – might pay Apple a visit.

Apple doesn't care about the store below or what it's charging. That store can serve the price-shoppers – those customers whose budgets are limited – because those customers are *not* Apple's customers. Instead, Apple invests its energy in making the service-shoppers – its fans – have an amazing experience. There are knowledgeable, passionate staff on hand, a Genius Bar, technicians out back who'll fix or replace a product in-store or replace it, and lots of lovely shiny stuff to play with while we wait.

Apple knows that there's room in the mall for both types of store and both types of customer. Editors need to recognize that it's the same for them.

Every teacup has a saucer

Remember Denise Cowle's Great Auntie Margaret? Every teacup has a saucer. There's room in the market for every editor and multiple pricing strategies because the market comprises every type of client with every type of budget and multiple motivations.

When Editor A argues that they believe no one will hire them because Editor B is charging 'unacceptably low rates' and driving a race to the bottom, A is assuming that all clients are the same. But they're not:

- Some clients will have lower incomes or busted cars that need expensive repairs, and they will be attracted to the editors who charge less (owing to a cost-based or democratic pricing strategy; or because they're experimenting with short-term discount or penetration pricing).

- Some will have more flexible budgets and will be focused first and foremost on finding the right-fit editor. Price will not be the clincher for this latter group; emotion will. They won't be deterred by premium value-based or inconvenience pricing. It might even attract them.

Being an Apple editor

If we don't want to compete with other editors on price, we need to get attention in a way that shifts the client's focus away from money and towards emotion so that they think: *That editor looks perfect for me, seems to get me, is really generous and knowledgeable. I hope she's available and that if I save up I can afford her.*

Yes, the price-focused clients won't touch us with a bargepole. But that's fine because we're not targeting them; we're targeting the value-focused clients. To be the Apple editor we need to present potential clients with an amazing experience – a story that says we have solutions, that we have their backs, that we can help them achieve their goals. A story that persuades them we're worth waiting for and worth paying for.

- It's about the words we use to convey our understanding of our clients' problems.
- It's about the images we use to convey our professional values. Blurry headshots with our mates or kids in them won't do.
- It's about how we instil trust. Telling them that we know our stuff – that we have the skills, the knowledge and the experience – is one thing. *Showing* them with free resources and a knowledge base that helps them more easily walk the publication path is quite another.

Summing up

Every minute we spend worrying about what other editors are charging is a minute we could devote to building our own compelling brand identity and creating our own valuable resources, stuff that helps our potential clients feel we're the right fit.

If you're invisible, it doesn't matter how high your prices are. No one will hire you. Not because your prices are too high but because you can't be seen. Being invisible is of no economic value to any editor.

If you want to compete on price, go ahead. If you want to compete on compulsion, go ahead. If you want to mix and match because different strategies fit better with particular client groups or types of project, go ahead. There is no race to the bottom. There's just a teacup looking for a saucer.

12. Protecting yourself

This chapter explores language and tools that help us repel those who'd let us down. The guidance will be more relevant to editors working with non-publisher/packager clients such as independent authors, students and businesses.

Language problems: 'Delay'

The concept of the delay is nonsense to an editorial business owner. If a client asks you to proofread a book, tells you the proofs will arrive with you on 10 May, and requests return of the marked-up proofs a week later, and you agree to take on the job, those are the terms: proofread starts 10 May; delivery 7 days later. You'll schedule the project accordingly, and will decline work from 10–17 May. If two weeks ahead of the start date you're told, 'There'll be a delay', you'll likely have no work for 10–17 May unless you can fill that space at the last minute. Moreover, you might already be booked for another project for the period when the 'delayed' project will become available.

Unless you can magic additional hours out of thin air, it's not a delay; it's a cancellation of the project terms that were agreed to by both parties. Make sure your T&Cs reflect this. Don't use the language of delay if it means nothing to you. Have a cancellation policy and make it clear that confirmed bookings are for an agreed time frame, and that failure to meet the agreed date will invoke that cancellation policy. Use the sample T&Cs in Appendix 1 as guidance if you wish.

Of course, you could decide not to invoke your cancellation policy as a courtesy, but having it could reduce the likelihood of having to make that decision in the first place.

Language problems: 'Deposit'

The word 'deposit' should be strong enough as long as the refund terms are clear. Still, you might want to couch your language along the lines of what editor and book coach Lisa Poisso calls 'real money'.

I don't refer to deposits in my terms and conditions. Instead, I call them booking fees. A fee is a payment. It's the language of money. 'Deposit' as a noun has a broader mass-of-material meaning; as a verb it means to place something somewhere. For some, it might have a softer feel to it. Of course, anyone required to pay a deposit knows full well that the financial definition is being referred to. Nevertheless, using the language of money – a fee – might encourage time-wasters to think twice.

Consider whether the following might also work for you:

- Down payment
- Advance payment
- Prepayment

What you charge upfront is up to you. Some editors charge a 50% booking fee rather than a flat rate. Some require one third to secure the booking, another third just before editing starts, and the remaining third upon completion of the project. You can define your own model.

Booking forms and contracts

Email agreements serve as contracts. But how about requiring a specific additional action, one that reinforces a sense of commitment? The booking form is one option to consider.

Asking someone to fill in a booking form that confirms they have read, understood and agreed to your terms and conditions, including your booking fee and your cancellation policy, means they have to make a proactive decision to commit. When it comes to filling in a form and ticking boxes, a non-committed client is less likely to feel comfortable than a good-fit one because the action feels more formal. There are different ways of going about it:

- Create a PDF booking form that you email to the client
- Add the form to your website

I've opted for a website booking form. It sits below my T&Cs. That way, the booking and the terms are closely linked.

Language problems: 'Booking form'

Even if a client is prepared to fill in a form and check some boxes, agreeing to a 'contract' might make them think twice. That has a more legally binding feel about it; it's more formal and might be the thing that repels someone who's going to let you down.

My T&Cs state that the booking-confirmation form is an agreement to the contract of services between me and the client. Furthermore, the phrase 'Contract of Services Agreement' sits under the title of the form.

The devil in the detail

When it comes to terms and conditions, forget all the touchy-feely stuff – this is where you and the client get down to business. It's in everyone's interests to know what's what. That might mean your T&Cs are rather dull and boring. No matter. It's the one place on your website where you're allowed to be dull and boring! I feel like chewing my own arm off when I read my T&Cs but I don't want any of my clients in doubt about what I'm offering and what they're getting. Consider the following:

- How much do you charge for a booking fee or advance payment?
- What are the penalties for cancellation and when do they kick in?
- Is final payment required before the edited project is delivered to the client?
- If you'll deliver first, will payment be required immediately? Within 7 days? Within 30 days?
- Are there penalties for late payment of the final invoice?
- Does your booking form require confirmation that your terms have been read, understood and agreed to?

A non-committed client will be repelled if your terms put them at risk. A good-fit client will feel reassured that they're dealing with a fellow professional who takes the editing work as seriously as they do.

Spotting red flags

While there's no foolproof way to protect yourself from non-committed clients, there are red flags you can look out for:

- The person tells you they want to go ahead and hire you for a specific time frame but doesn't fill in the booking form, or you have to nudge them several times. This could indicate that they're not yet committed to working with you.

- The person fills in the booking form but fails to pay your booking fee. This could indicate that the funds are not in place, and might never be.
- The person fills in a booking form and pays the fee but seeks to change the terms they booked under. This might indicate that they're not in the right mindset to commit to your editing services.
- The person is consistently slow to respond to emails during the initial discussion phase, and needs frequent nudging about the state of play. This might indicate that they don't take your business offering seriously.
- The person gives you conflicting information about what's required, or repeats questions about money and dates that you've already answered. This indicates they've not read your correspondence properly, which could lead to problems later.
- The person hasn't begun the writing process, or has but isn't sure when they'll finish. If you don't keep in regular touch with the client to check the project's on track – which is time-consuming – the project could go off the rails and you'll be none the wiser.

Summing up

Most clients are honest, committed and trustworthy. As for those who blow you out, a few are scoundrels. Others are just thoughtless and haven't taken the time to understand the emotional and financial impact of cancellations and non-payment. Yet others have got cold feet. And some have been struck by unusual or extraordinary circumstances such as bereavement. Most don't mean to cause distress or financial hardship, even though those are two very real potential outcomes for editors.

By using real-money language and action-driving tools, we can build stronger bonds of trust with those who are serious about working with us, and repel most of those who aren't.

13. No price is perfect

No matter which pricing strategy we choose, we won't always hit the mark.

The day before I finished writing this guide, an indie fiction author asked me to quote for line editing an 86,000-word eco-thriller. I offered £30 per 1,000 words. She replied saying the quote 'seemed perfectly reasonable' as long as I could complete the work within three months. One of my clients had cancelled because lockdown had affected his writing. I was sad for him but pleased to fill the slot. Two hours after the eco-thriller writer confirmed the booking, another author asked me to quote for an 87,000-word crime novel. I offered him the same per-word price and he came back to me within minutes saying my fee was beyond his budget. I wished him well. Some you win; some you lose.

It doesn't matter that every potential client's expectations won't be in line with our fees. All that matters is that *enough* clients are willing to pay what we want to earn. That's not about finding a perfect price; it's about getting our branding and marketing in place so that we're visible to those for whom we're a good fit. A pricing strategy is therefore part of a marketing strategy. And while there's no single best way to be discoverable (because the approaches we favour will be determined by the types of clients we want to work with) we must do *something* to ensure that we can be seen and valued by those who'll commission us.

Don't try to find a price that will be perfect for every client now. Instead, think about your needs and goals, now and in the future, and the pricing models that are best aligned with your circumstances. Test the water, record the data and review your decisions at least annually.

And remember, what anyone else thinks about your pricing is irrelevant. What matters is that your rates work for you.

Appendix 1: Terms and conditions template

Feel free to copy and tweak this template for your business. Read it carefully and make any relevant and necessary adjustments.

Terms and conditions: Contract of proofreading/editing services

The following terms and conditions are provided so that you and I both have an upfront and honest understanding of what is involved in the process of working together. If you have any questions or concerns, feel free to contact me so that I can provide clarity and reassurance.

1. General overview

1.1 These terms and conditions apply to any work done on behalf of the Client (you) by me ([insert your business name]).

1.2 I will provide proofreading/editing services agreed upon (in writing) by myself and the Client.

1.3 The Client is under no obligation to offer me work; neither am I under any obligation to accept work offered by the Client.

1.4 The work will be carried out unsupervised at such times and places as determined by me, using my own equipment.

1.5 The work will be carried out by me. I will not subcontract proofreading/editing projects, or parts of projects, to third parties.

1.6 I confirm that I am self-employed, am responsible for my own income tax and National Insurance contributions, and will not claim benefits granted to the Client's employees.

1.7 I am not VAT-registered.

1.8 The contract of service requires that the Client acknowledges, in writing (including email via the booking-confirmation form), that they have read, understood and agreed to these terms and conditions.

2. Project terms

2.1 Prior to commencement of the proofreading/editing work, the Client and I will agree, in writing (including email), the terms of the project:

- the medium in which the proofreading/editing service will be carried out (e.g. in Word, on PDF, on paper)
- how the material will be annotated (e.g. Track Changes in Word, BSI correction symbols on paper)
- the length of time required to complete the project, as advised by me
- a fee for the project, based on a quotation supplied by me, in writing (including email), following my evaluation of the material to be proofread/edited and the time frame required to complete the job
- any expenses (e.g. postage) that the Client will bear in addition to the costs of the proofreading/editing
- the date by which the material will be delivered by the Client to me
- the latest date by which the completed project will be returned, following my advice to the Client
-

2.2 Please note that if, on receipt of the project to be worked on (or at an early stage), it becomes apparent that significantly more work is required than had been anticipated in the preliminary discussion/brief or from the sample supplied, I may renegotiate the fee and/or the deadline, or decline to carry out the work.

3. Quotations and fees

3.1 A quotation for the work will be provided by me to the Client following my evaluation of a representative sample of the materials to be worked on, and a discussion with the Client as to what is required.

3.2 Once the Client and I have agreed the full fee, it is non-negotiable unless the Client extends the word count of the job or requests additional services. In this case, a revised quotation and job-completion date will be negotiated.

3.3 The Client will pay me a fee per 1,000 words OR per hour OR an agreed flat fee for the project, as agreed in writing.

3.4 Unless otherwise agreed, I will supply the Client with an invoice immediately upon completion of the proofreading/editing project.

3.5 Payment should be received within 14 days for full edits, and within 3 days for booking fees.

3.6 I am a signatory to the Pay On Time code of practice [add link].

3.7 Unless otherwise agreed, the fee quoted is for one pass of a manuscript. Additional passes are new projects, the terms of which will be agreed separately.

4. Booking-confirmation form

4.1 The booking-confirmation form is an agreement to the contract of services between me and the Client.

5. Booking fee

5.1 When the Client has sent the booking-confirmation form at the bottom of this page, I will issue the invoice for the booking fee.

5.2 Booking fees are non-refundable.

5.3 For a project with a total fee in excess of £500, the Client will pay a booking fee of £500.

5.4 For a project with a total fee of £500 or less, the Client will pay the full fee up front. This is non-refundable.

5.5 By filling in the booking-confirmation form, the Client agrees to secure my proofreading/editing services for a specific and mutually agreed-upon project, at a specific and mutually agreed time.

5.6 By filling in the booking-confirmation form, the Client confirms that they have read and agreed to the terms and conditions herein. From thereon, the terms of the cancellation policy (see below) apply.

5.7 The booking fee will be deducted from the final invoice issued when the editing work is complete.

5.8 The booking is considered confirmed once the booking fee has been paid by the Client and received by me.

5.9 The booking fee should be paid within 3 days of sending the booking-confirmation form to secure the slot in my schedule.

6. Cancellation policy: Terms, fees and project-commencement reminders

TERMS:

6.1 Both the Client and I have the right to terminate a contract for services at any time if there is a serious breach of its terms.

6.2 This Client is free to cancel a service for any reason by providing me with written notice (including email); I must acknowledge this cancellation in writing (including email) for this to be valid.

6.3 I may cancel a service at any time for any reason by providing written notice (including email) to the Client. In the unlikely event that I cancel a service, I will provide a prorated refund of any overages of fees paid (including the booking fee).

6.4 If, in the unlikely event that the Client is touched by extraordinary or difficult circumstances that cause cancellation or delay (e.g. family crisis, illness, bereavement), the Client should contact me to discuss the terms of the cancellation policy. I aim to be fair and helpful at all times.

6.5 If I am touched by extraordinary or difficult circumstances that cause cancellation (e.g. family crisis, illness, bereavement), I will contact the Client in writing at the earliest opportunity and do my best to renegotiate the time frame of the project or find an alternative supplier of proofreading/editing services. The booking fee will be refunded.

FEES:

6.6 Cancellation during the project: If the Client cancels the work during the proofreading/editing project, I reserve the right to invoice for 100% of the agreed fee (less the booking fee).

6.7 Cancellation prior to project commencement: If the Client wishes to cancel with less than one month's notice, I reserve the right to invoice for 100% of the agreed fee (less the booking fee).

If the Client wishes to cancel with more than one month's notice, the booking fee will not be refunded but no other charge will apply.

PROJECT-COMMENCEMENT REMINDERS:

6.8 I will contact the Client two weeks before the mutually agreed start date with a reminder that the file is due 24 hours before said start date.

If in the unlikely event that the Client does not confirm in writing (including email) within one week prior to the mutually agreed start date that they will be supplying the file for editing, the project is deemed to have been cancelled by the Client and the slot in my schedule will be released.

If, as is likely, the Client confirms the project, I will ask for the file to be sent to me 24 hours before the start date.

7. Confidentiality

7.1 The nature and content of the work will be kept confidential and not made known to anyone other than the Client and its contractors without prior written permission.

7.2 I will not, under any circumstances, upload the Client's files to external websites or distribute them to third parties unless specifically authorized to do so, in writing, by the Client. I do, however, use [your provider] as a cloud storage system. See my Privacy Policy [add link] for how your data is protected.

7.3 Under the terms of the Data Protection Act 1998, the Client and I may keep on record such information (e.g. contact details) as is necessary. Either may view the other's records to ensure that they are relevant, correct and up to date.

8. Copyright

8.1 All content delivered to me by the Client for the proofreading or editing project is owned by the Client.

8.2 In this respect, the Client agrees to hold me harmless from and against all claims, liabilities and expenses arising out of any potential or actual copyright or trademark misappropriation or infringement claimed against them.

8.3 Following payment of my invoice, any content created by me as part of the proofreading/editing process will become the copyright of the Client unless otherwise agreed.

9. Legal jurisdiction

9.1 This agreement is subject to the laws of [your jurisdiction], and both the Client and I agree to submit to the jurisdiction of the [your jurisdiction] courts.

9.2 The exclusive venue for any arbitration or court proceeding based on or arising out of this Agreement shall be [your city, country].

10. Privacy policy and the GDPR

10.1 Please read my Privacy Policy, which explains the data I collect, how I use it and store it, and my compliance with the General Data Protection Regulation (GDPR).

11. Acknowledgements in published works

11.1 There is no requirement for the Client to mention me in the published work's acknowledgements section. However, the Client agrees that I will have the opportunity to review any such mention prior to publication, or to decline to be mentioned.

Appendix 2: Privacy policy template

Feel free to copy this template for your business. Read it carefully and make any relevant and necessary adjustments.

Privacy policy

I am a registered sole trader operating as [Your Business Name]. I offer [your services] to [your clients]. My client/customer base is worldwide.

This policy describes how I protect and make use of the information you give me.

If you are asked to provide information, it will only be used in ways stated in this policy.

This privacy policy was last updated on [date].

Why do I collect data from you?

I gather and use certain information about you in order to:

- respond to your requests for information (e.g. my availability or a quote for editorial services)
- allow you to register for a special offer
- allow me to contact you while an editing project is ongoing
- enable certain functions on this website
- better understand how visitors use this website

What information do I collect from you?

I collect the following minimal information:

- name
- contact postal address
- email address
- information pertinent to your enquiry (e.g. word count, nature of project, whether you're an author or an editor)

How do I use this data?

The data I collect is used as follows:

- For my internal accounting processes (e.g. so I can invoice you) and so that I am compliant with my tax authority [(Name of Your Tax Authority) should it request an audit.
- To contact you in response to your enquiry, order, quote, special offer or booking.
- To give you access to content you have purchased that resides on my website.
- To record your agreement to the terms and conditions of my editorial services.

I will never use this data for marketing or promotion purposes without getting your permission in writing first (for example, to publish your testimonial for me on my website), or unless you have signed up to be notified about a specific offer.

How do I use cookies?

A cookie is a small file placed on your computer's hard drive. It enables my website to identify your computer as you view different pages on my website.

The only way in which I use cookies is for web analytics, specifically [web analytics provider].

Cookies do not provide me with access to your computer or any information about you other than that which you elect to share with me.

You can use your web browser's cookie settings to determine how my website uses cookies. If you do not want my website to store cookies on your computer or device, you can amend your settings. Please note that this may affect how my website functions, and some pages may become unavailable to you.

- To learn more about cookies, visit All About Cookies [add link].
- To read [web analytics provider's] privacy statement, and how you can request that I remove your information from my analytics data, see [web analytics provider's] data privacy policies and approach [add link] and its data processing terms [add link].

How do I collect your personal data?

I collect and store minimal information via the following forms:

- Contact form (via [your host])
- Booking-confirmation form (via [your host])
- Course/book order form (via [your host])
- Author's style preferences form (via [your host])
- Newsletter signup (via [your provider])
- Email (via [your provider])

I will never lease, distribute or sell your information to third parties unless you give me written permission to do so, or I am required to do so by law.

You can ask me to remove your data from [your host] or [your provider] at any time. Please note that if your information is being held to enable access to content that you've purchased from me (e.g. courses/books), the removal of your data will remove your access.

How do I store your personal data?

The minimal information I collect is stored on the following data servers:

- [Your host]. This is my website host. It is password-protected and has SSL-certification (https) to provide an additional layer of security. You can access [your host's] privacy policy here [add link].
- [Your provider]. This is my cloud-based file management system accessed via my password-protected computer. My [your provider] account is protected by a two-step password-authentication process. You can access its privacy policy here [add link].
- [Your provider]. This is my blog-subscription management system. [Your provider] requires a double opt-in. That means that after a subscriber signs up they have to confirm their opt-in via email. You can access its privacy policy here [add link].
- [Ecommerce provider]. This is the password-protected online payment service I use for sales of my courses and books, and for editorial-services clients who elect not to be invoiced via direct bank transfer.

- [Your provider]. This is the [your country]-based password-protected server I use to communicate via email. You can access its privacy policy here [add link].
- [Your provider]. This is the accounting app I use to send invoices. Your name, email address and a project summary are stored. You can access its privacy policy here[add link], its security policy here [add link], and its terms of use here [add link].

DATA SERVERS IN THE UNITED STATES

- [Your website host], [your cloud storage system] and [your mailing list provider] servers are based in the US but are registered with the EU–US Privacy Shield [add link].
- All [your ecommerce provider] transactions are subject to the its Privacy Policy [add link]. Your data will used for accounting purposes only and will never be divulged to third parties.

How long do I keep your data for?

Because many of my customers and clients work with me more than once, I do not delete data unless specifically requested to do so.

- [Your tax authority] requires me to keep records for [insert relevant time period].
- Please ask if you want me to delete or amend your records. As long as I'm complying with [your tax authority's] legal requirements, I'll action your request immediately.

With whom is your data shared?

No one, unless you request that I do so in writing, or [your tax authority] elects to audit my business.

Contact me

If you have any questions or requests for modification or removal of your data, you are welcome to email me at [your email address] or write to me at [your name and address].

If you need assistance with creating your own GDPR-compliant website privacy policy, the ICO [add link] provides some excellent guidance.

Resources

- Calconic: 'A Step-By-Step Guide to Building an Instant Quote Calculator for Your Website', https://bit.ly/2ZscdlK
- Celine Roque, 'Why You Shouldn't Just Give a Quote to Potential Clients', Gigaom, 2008: https://gigaom.com/2008/05/05/why-you-shouldnt-just-give-a-quote-to-potential-clients/
- Clockify: https://clockify.me
- ConvertCalculator: https://www.convertcalculator.co
- Do, Chris, 'Pricing Design Work & Creativity', YouTube, 2016: https://bit.ly/3dmVdCg
- Editing macros from Paul Beverley: www.archivepub.co.uk/macros
- Excel Scheduling Template: https://harnby.co/excel-schedule
- How to Write the Perfect Editorial Report (multimedia course): https://harnby.co/report-course
- PDF proofreading stamps: https://harnby.co/PDF-stamps
- PerfectIt: https://intelligentediting.com/
- Steve Payne, 'Sales 101: Don't Get to Price Too Early, Even If You're Asked to "Ballpark"', Sexton Group Ltd, 2015: http://sextongroup.com/sales-101-dont-get-price-early-even-youre-asked-ballpark/
- TextExpander: https://textexpander.com/
- The Editor's Affairs: https://www.whatimeantosay.com/tea.html
- Thompson, Melanie, *Pricing a Project: How to Prepare a Professional Quotation*, Chartered Institute of Editing and Proofreading (CIEP)
- Toggl: https://toggl.com

Glossary of pricing strategies

Bundle: Offering a single price for multiple services.

Client-offer: Accepting or declining a client's price.

Competitor-based: Assessing what your competitors are charging, and pricing similarly.

Cost-based: Making something and selling it for more than the costs of production.

Customer-based: Setting rates according to a perceived ceiling on the price your target clients will bear.

Democratic: Pricing at a level that's purposefully designed not to exclude particular communities but is still profitable.

Discount: Reducing price with the aim of bringing the client on board at a higher rate in the future.

Inconvenience: Charging a fee that's higher than your standard rate because the client wants the work done at a time or in a place that's undesirable.

Loss leader: Offering a low or no price on some services in the hope of persuading the client to buy a higher-priced service.

Pay-what-you-want: Asking the client for a donation.

Penetration: Temporarily offering your services at a low entry price.

Predatory: Knocking all your competitors out of the market, then raising your prices and monopolizing the now empty-but-for-you market.

Retainer: Charging for a client's right to use your services for an agreed number of hours, whether or not the client actually provides you with any work.

Risk-based: Setting fees based not just on the value of your time but also on the risk the client attaches to *not* hiring you.

Tiered: Pricing that factors in economies of scale.

Value-based: Setting prices according to the perceived value of your products or services in the market.

Printed in Great Britain
by Amazon